BOB MARLEY

BOB MARLEY

A Biography

David V. Moskowitz

GREENWOOD BIOGRAPHIES

GREENWOOD PRESS
WESTPORT, CONNECTICUT • LONDON

Library of Congress Cataloging-in-Publication Data

Moskowitz, David V. (David Vlado), 1969–
    Bob Marley : a biography / David V. Moskowitz.
        p. cm. — (Greenwood biographies, ISSN 1540-4900)
    Discography: p.
    Includes bibliographical references and index.
    ISBN-13: 978–0–313–33879–3 (alk. paper)
    ISBN-10: 0–313–33879–5 (alk. paper)
    1.   Marley, Bob. 2.   Reggae musicians—Jamaica—Biography.   I. Title.
    ML420.M3313M66   2007
    782.421646092—dc22
    [B]   2007018313

British Library Cataloguing in Publication Data is available.

Library of Congress Catalog Card Number: 2007018313
ISBN-13: 978–0–313–33879–3
ISBN-10: 0–313–33879–5
ISSN: 1540–4900

First published in 2007

Greenwood Press, 88 Post Road West, Westport, CT 06881
An imprint of Greenwood Publishing Group, Inc.
www.greenwood.com

Printed in the United States of America

The paper used in this book complies with the
Permanent Paper Standard issued by the National
Information Standards Organization (Z39.48–1984).

10   9   8   7   6   5   4   3   2   1

For Jack, welcome to the world

CONTENTS

Photo essay follows page 66

SERIES FOREWORD

In response to high school and public library needs, Greenwood developed this distinguished series of full-length biographies specifically for student use. Prepared by field experts and professionals, these engaging biographies are tailored for high school students who need challenging yet accessible biographies. Ideal for secondary school assignments, the length, format and subject areas are designed to meet educators' requirements and students' interests.

Greenwood offers an extensive selection of biographies spanning all curriculum related subject areas including social studies, the sciences, literature and the arts, history and politics, as well as popular culture, covering public figures and famous personalities from all time periods and backgrounds, both historic and contemporary, who have made an impact on American and/or world culture. Greenwood biographies were chosen based on comprehensive feedback from librarians and educators. Consideration was given to both curriculum relevance and inherent interest. The result is an intriguing mix of the well known and the unexpected, the saints and sinners from long-ago history and contemporary pop culture. Readers will find a wide array of subject choices from fascinating crime figures like Al Capone to inspiring pioneers like Margaret Mead, from the greatest minds of our time like Stephen Hawking to the most amazing success stories of our day like J. K. Rowling.

While the emphasis is on fact, not glorification, the books are meant to be fun to read. Each volume provides in-depth information about the subject's life from birth through childhood, the teen years, and adulthood.

A thorough account relates family background and education, traces personal and professional influences, and explores struggles, accomplishments, and contributions. A timeline highlights the most significant life events against a historical perspective. Bibliographies supplement the reference value of each volume.

ACKNOWLEDGMENTS

My sincerest thanks go to my wife, Jen, and our children Heather, Lucas, Katie, and Jack. Without their boundless patience there would never be enough time for me to work on projects such as this. Thanks also go to Dr. Walter Clark whose guidance and tutelage have helped me to pursue the research that interests me most. Further thanks to Photofest Inc. for their kind permission to use the images contained in this book.

TIMELINE: EVENTS IN THE LIFE OF BOB MARLEY

1945   Nesta Robert Marley, the only child of Cedella Malcolm and Captain Norval Sinclair Marley, was born at 2:30 P.M. on February 6, 1945. The birth took place on Cedella's father's (Omeriah Malcolm's) farm in Nine Mile, St. Ann's Parish, Jamaica. Bob stayed on this family farm until he was six.

1951   Bob went to live with his father in Kingston, Jamaica. When Cedella arrived the following year to look in on Bob, she discovered that he had not been living with his father but had instead been staying with an elderly woman named Mrs. Grey.

1952   Once mother and son were reunited, they returned together to their rural Jamaican home in St. Ann.

1955   Bob learned that his father had died, his mother moved to Kingston (without him) to earn a better living.

1956   Bob was moved from his grandfather's farm to live with his mother's sister, for whom he tended a herd of goats.

1957   Bob was reunited with his mother when he moved to Kingston to join her. This otherwise happy reunion was marred by the fact that they now lived in Kingston's west-side ghetto known as Trench Town.

1959   After attending several area schools, including Ebenezer, Wesley, and St. Aloysius, Bob ended his formal education when he quit school. He spent his time playing

soccer, hanging out with other ghetto youth, and gradually picking up music.

1960   Together with his closest friend Bunny, born Neville
Livingston, Bob began to cultivate his musical talents.
He and Bunny built rudimentary instruments and together they practiced singing by imitating Fats Domino,
Louis Jordan, and the harmonies of Curtis Mayfield's Impressions. Also during this year, Bob and Bunny began
studying singing with the Jamaican recording artist Joe
Higgs. Higgs not only provided singing lessons, but he
added Peter Tosh (born MacIntosh) to the group.

1962   At age 16, Bob was taken to sing for producer Leslie
Kong, who issued his first recordings, "Judge Not," "One
Cup of Coffee," and "Terror," on the Beverley's imprint.

1963   Bob, Peter, and Bunny recorded for Clement "Coxsone"
Dodd, who was one of the three biggest producers of
Jamaican popular music on the island. Under the name
The Wailing Wailers, the group released the single
"Simmer Down," which brought them considerable suc-
cess in Jamaica.

1965   The Wailing Wailers continued to have success with
a series of solid-selling singles. By the end of the year,
it was clear that Bob was the natural front man for the
group. This led to friction that ultimately broke up the
original three-member group. Early in the year, Bob
met Rita Anderson (Alpharita Constantia Anderson),
whom he soon married.

1966   Together, Bob and Rita had three children, although
Bob had many other children outside his relationship
with Rita. Later in this year, Bob moved to Wilmington, Delaware. Bob remained in Wilmington for seven
months, during which time he worked a variety of odd
jobs trying to make enough money to launch his own
Jamaica-based record company. While in Wilmington, Bob stayed with his mother, who had previously
relocated to the United States.

1969   Bob, Peter, and Bunny (under the name of the Wailers)
recorded a series of successful singles for Johnny Nash
and Danny Sims's JAD label. In the middle of the year,
Bob was again in Delaware making and saving money to
open his own studio in Jamaica.

1970   The Wailers begin recording a series of now classic
       singles for producer Lee "Scratch" Perry in what would
       be a legendary lineup: Bob Marley, Bunny Wailer, Peter
       Tosh, and the Barrett Brothers (Aston and Carlton) as
       the rhythm section.
1971   Bob, Peter, and Bunny, along with their rhythm section
       Aston and Carlton Barrett, were in London working for
       Nash and Sims on a record deal for CBS records. At the
       end of the year, the group was abandoned in London
       with no means to return to Jamaica. Bob made contact
       with Island Records' head, Christopher Blackwell, who
       fronted him the money to get the band back to Jamaica
       and make an album. This association quickly made Is-
       land Records the most important reggae music label.
1972   The Wailers released *Catch a Fire*, which was the first
       album-length recording of reggae music. The album had
       modest success and a degree of crossover appeal due to
       the rock and roll style guitar and keyboard overdubs that
       Blackwell added to the original tracks. In January 1973,
       the album was released in the United States and forever
       changed the way that reggae music was packaged and
       marketed. *Catch a Fire* was soon universally recognized
       as the first genuine reggae album in history.
1973   The Wailers launched their first official tour, which
       included television appearances on the *Old Grey Whistle
       Test* and *Top Gear*. Also in this year, the Wailers released
       their second record on the Island label, *Burnin'*.
1974   The Wailers reached international exposure due to Eric
       Clapton's cover of the Wailers song "I Shot the Sheriff."
       The song went to number one and sparked an enormous
       amount of interest in the reggae style. While they were
       experiencing the most success they had yet had, the
       original three-member Wailers core disbanded. Bob
       continued to use the Wailers name for the rest of his
       life. Without Peter and Bunny, Bob went on to release
       the *Natty Dread* album at the end of the year.
1975   In January, the original Wailers officially disbanded. The
       Natty Dread album was released internationally in Feb-
       ruary. Much of the summer and fall of the year was taken
       up by an international tour in support of the new album.
       Several shows were recorded in England and made into

the first Wailers concert album, called *Live!* The album sold well in the UK and was released in the United States in 1976.

1976   Bob appeared on the cover of *Rolling Stone* magazine. Bob Marley and the Wailers released the *Rastaman Vibration* album then toured for three months to support the release. At approximately 8:45 P.M. on December 3, gunmen broke into Marley's house at 56 Hope Road and opened fire. Bob and Rita were each shot once and their manager, Don Taylor, was shot several times. Everyone survived, but this forced Bob into self-imposed exile in fear for his life.

1977   In the wake of the assassination attempt, Bob released a flurry of records. *Exodus* was issued on June 3, 1977.

1978   *Kaya* album released in early 1978. The *Exodus* and *Kaya* releases both spawned successful tours. Bob set up the Jamaican Peace Concert, which featured several important reggae acts. The concert was produced to help settle some of the violence that had been tearing the island apart.

1979   Bob and the Wailers released the *Survival* album in October of 1979. The album was another big success and led to another international tour which was launched in Boston at the end of October.

1980   The sessions that produced the *Survival* material also yielded the songs for the album *Uprising*. *Uprising* was released in June and was supported by another international tour with dates in the United States and Western Europe, during which the Wailers played for over one million people. During the North American leg of the *Uprising* tour, Bob collapsed while jogging in New York's Central Park. It was soon discovered that he had suffered a stroke and the rest of the tour was canceled. The last live show that Bob Marley and the Wailers played was on September 23, 1980, at Pittsburgh's Stanley Theater. In the wake of his collapse, Bob was diagnosed with terminal cancer in his stomach, lungs, and brain. At the end of the year, Bob traveled to Bad Wiessee, Germany, seeking nontraditional cancer treatment from Dr. Josef Issels. Dr. Issels was able to extend Bob's life, but could not successfully treat the cancer.

1980   On October 4, American popular musician Stevie Won-
        der released a tribute to the cancer-stricken reggae su-
        perstar. The song was reggae-like in style and was called
        "Master Blaster (Jammin')." It went on to be a serious
        hit on the U.S. rhythm and blues charts and topped out
        at number five on the pop charts.

1981   At 11:45 on Monday, May 11, 1981, Robert Nesta
        Marley, the first third-world musician who rose to inter-
        national super stardom, died. In death, Bob was treated
        as a Jamaican national hero. He was awarded Jamaica's
        National Order of Merit and given a state funeral.
        Afterward, Bob's body was taken to his St. Ann's birth-
        place where it remains. Since his death, Bob's childhood
        home in St. Ann and his house at 56 Hope Road have
        become places of pilgrimage for ardent fans. Although
        there are many albums that have been released after
        Bob's death, the *Confrontation* album (released in 1983)
        was the only posthumous release that was conceived of
        by Bob before he died.

1984   The most popular collection of Bob's greatest hits, *Leg-
        end*, was released. The album went on to become the
        highest-selling reggae album of all time.

1999   The collection of Bob's greatest hits, *Legend*, received its
        10th platinum certification, signifying that it had sold
        more than 10 million copies. This continues to easily
        hold the record for the highest-selling reggae boxed set.

Chapter 1

COUNTRY BOY TO GHETTO YOUTH

Robert Nesta Marley was the first and possibly the only superstar to emerge from the third world. From his meager rural beginnings, Bob blossomed into a man of such significant import and influence that his attempted assassination in 1976 was politically motivated. Bob's musical influence is still felt. His was the first reggae act to release a full-length LP, which immediately changed the marketing model that had existed for 30 years. Beyond its commercial impact, Bob's music has a universal quality that transcends race, color, economic class, even language. For example, it is known that his music is listened to by such diverse groups as the Maori people of New Zealand and the Hopi Indians living in America's Grand Canyon.

Although he lived a short life, only 36 years, Bob penned an enormous quantity of songs. And unlike some songwriters, Bob was involved in all aspects of the creation of his music. He worked on each of the instrumental parts, wrote the lyrics, and had his hand in the control room while the initial tracks were being laid down, in addition to being involved in the editing and overdubbing process that yielded the final product. Bob's sound was so characteristic of reggae that it virtually cornered the "roots reggae" designation. His rhythm section pioneered the standard roots reggae groove, which they called "one drop" rhythm. One drop rhythm was achieved when the drummer accented only the third beat of a four beat measure. The classical music of Western Europe typically accented the first and the third beat in a four beat measure, and American rock and roll music emphasized beats two and four. This unique reggae rhythm separated it from the music from which it grew and made it distinctly Jamaican in character. Bob so liked this style of playing that he wrote a song that illustrated the rhythm (the song is called "One Drop") and included lyrics about the fine quality of this rhythm. In addition to his achievements in forming the reggae sound, Bob was also an expert lyricist. The equal of any contemporary hip-hop word slinger, Bob was able to craft emotionally powerful chains of words that are pleasing to listen to on the surface but that pack a serious punch when their meanings are explored. He was able to draw the meaning and the emotion out of each word and then expertly hide them in relaxed "island"-sounding music. Bob did this on purpose. If his music was too overtly political or venomous, it would not be commercial or radio friendly. Bob also knew his way around a good rock and roll song. His music is often delivered in the standard verse/chorus form with additional weight added to the chorus material. This is a time-honored rock and roll form with roots from Elvis to the Beatles.

Regardless of Bob's poverty-stricken childhood, his adult life contained the trappings of success. At the height of his career in the late 1970s, Bob lived in a big house in downtown Kingston, the capital city of Jamaica. The house contained all of the standard living spaces, plus rehearsal and recording spaces so that Bob and his band could work where they lived. A typical day at this house, 56 Hope Road, was to spend the morning playing soccer and smoking ganja (Jamaican slang for marijuana), the afternoon conducting business and meeting with people who often wanted Bob to give them money, and the evening rehearsing and recording, continuing well into the night. Bob did acquire some of the symbols of a wealthy person. For example, he drove a BMW, which was certainly an indication of his monetary standing. However, Bob did not really care much for such symbols and reportedly bought the car because BMW could stand for Bob Marley and the Wailers. Like his childhood home in St. Ann's Parish, the house at 56 Hope Road has been converted into a museum. The upstairs bedrooms are now gallery space that house items such as a large map of the world with push pins marking all of the places where Bob and the Wailers toured. Bob's son Ziggy's old room (his son's actual name is David) has been made into a business office and a library. Bob's master bedroom is also on the second floor and it has been preserved just the way that it was when he died.

As well as the attraction that Bob's music had, he also had a very magnetic personality. Bob was described as open, honest, and approachable, especially to his ghetto brothers and sisters. However, when deceived by a business associate or cornered by an interviewer, Bob could become quite nasty; he would quickly give the person a serious look that made everyone understand that he should not be taken for granted. Another way that

Bob separated himself from the Western world was in his speech. While English is the official language of Jamaica, most Jamaicans actually speak a pidgin version of the language including words adopted from various African languages and a great deal of slang. So, if Bob wanted to be understood he spoke in plain English, but if he wanted to confuse the person he was talking to or wanted to purposely obscure his meaning, then he switched into a thick Jamaican accent that was completely unintelligible to anyone who was not from the island.

As a professional performer, Bob presented a kind of front that manifested itself in the way he acted and the way he looked. He favored denim shirts and pants, boots, and stocking hats (called tams). On stage he often fell into a trance-like state while singing. He would keep his eyes closed and flail his arms while swinging his long dreadlocks. All of these components together created Bob Marley the legend.

Bob's impact was felt during his life and continues to be felt today. Since 1991, Bob Marley and the Wailers have sold in excess of 21 million records (these statistics did not begin to be collected until 10 years after his death). Further, Bob has a star on the Hollywood Walk of Fame, he was inducted into the Rock and Roll Hall of Fame, he received the Grammy Lifetime Achievement Award, and he was awarded the Jamaican Order of Merit. Regardless of these (and many other) awards, the true test of Bob's worth is time. Twenty-five years after his death, the music of Bob Marley and the Wailers is as popular, important, and pertinent as it was the day it was released.

JAMAICA

Jamaica is one of the larger Caribbean islands and is located about two hundred miles south of the islands at the southern tip of Florida (the Florida Keys). The island itself is little more than a mountain sticking up through the surface of the ocean; however, due to its climate Jamaica is an island paradise. The low-lying coastal areas contain the majority of the island's population, and the majority of the people living in the interior have traditionally lived off the land. In fact, much of the Jamaican economy has been based on the exportation of their crops, such as coffee, sugarcane, bananas, coconuts, citrus fruits, and pimento. The population of the island is sparse in its interior, but quite dense in the cities of Kingston (the capital), Montego Bay, Negril, and Ocho Rios. An interesting duality on the island is the great disparity between the wealthy and the poor. Jamaica is still part of the third world as many of its inhabitants do not have running water, electricity, or telephone service. Conversely, the island's cites are as modern as any in the United States. This economic divide also creates an unstable environment that is often marked by political unrest and violence. It was into these circumstances that Nesta Robert (the order of his names was later reversed) Marley was born at 2:30 P.M. on February 6, 1945.

BIRTH IN NINE MILE

Bob was born in the rural interior of the island in a parish called St. Ann. Jamaican parishes are vaguely equivalent to counties in the United States. Bob was born to a black Jamaican mother, Cedella Malcolm, and a white Jamaican father, Captain Norval Sinclair (or Saint Clair) Marley. The two were an odd pair as Cedella was only 18 and Norval, a member of the British army, was in his early sixties. Bob's birth took place on his maternal grandfather's farm. Omeriah Malcolm was a landowning black man who was a respected inhabitant of the village called Nine Mile. Bob's birthplace is a small rural community that is located high in the interior mountains of the island. Bob's mother and father had met on Omeriah's farm, and the two were married there on June 9, 1944. The wedding was not the usual happy occasion, as Captain Marley announced that he would be departing Nine Mile the following day. He had been offered a government job in Kingston and had no intention of returning to St. Ann. The captain did return, however, on the occasion of Bob's birth. After a week's stay, the captain again returned to Kingston and gradually lost touch with his wife and son.

Because the captain was not taking financial responsibility for his new family, Cedella had to support her son. Her father allowed her to open a small grocery store on the family property where she could sell the crops that she helped grow. There is some disagreement about Cedella and Bob's care during his early life. Stephen Davis noted in his biography of the reggae superstar that Captain Marley left Omeriah with enough money to build Cedella and Bob a small cabin to live in and startup money for the grocery store. Regardless, Cedella and Bob were poor and barely scraping by at this time. While Bob was still a baby, the captain contacted Cedella to request that she send Bob to Kingston to live with him. Bob's mother wanted no part of this separation from her child; however, the captain did not let the issue drop completely.

Bob began his formal education at age four when he began attending the Stepney School. Stepney was a basic school and provided Bob with rudimentary education in letters and numbers. During his early education, Bob was singled out by his teacher as being a bright child and a fast learner. When Bob was six years old, his father reappeared in Nine Mile and again tried to convince Cedella that Bob would be better off in Kingston. This time, his father added that Bob's education would be better served at the bigger, better Kingston public school. Cedella and Omeriah considered the captain's request and decided that it was in Bob's best interest to attend school in Kingston. Further, Cedella could not afford Bob's school clothes and lunches. All this having been considered, Bob went to Kingston to live with his father and attend public school.

Cedella and the captain corresponded during her separation from her son and she was always reassured that Bob was doing well. After six months, Cedella planned to ride the bus into Kingston to visit her son. The captain put her off, saying that Bob was away on a school trip and this evasion foreshadowed Captain Marley's deceit. After a full year had passed, Cedella had had enough of the captain's stalling. She had learned from a friend that Bob was not in fact living with the captain at all. She had also been told that Bob was unhappy with his Kingston arrangements and was waiting for his mother's assistance.

In early 1952, Cedella arrived in Kingston to reclaim her son. This presented a problem as she no longer knew where the captain or Bob lived. Cedella had received word that Bob was likely living on Heywood Street, so she went there and began asking about her son. Soon she learned that Bob had been living with an elderly woman named Mrs. Grey, and as Cedella searched out Mrs. Grey's house, around the corner came Bob. Reunited with his mother, Bob took her to meet Mrs. Grey, who informed Cedella that Bob had been living with her since his arrival in Kingston. The captain's plan was that by living with Mrs. Grey, Bob would become her heir when she died. With the captain's plan exposed and foiled, Bob and Cedella returned to St. Ann.

Back in his rural birthplace, Bob again studied at the Stepney School. While not studying, Bob helped his mother run the grocery store. While working at the store Bob began to exhibit his singing talent. His mother reported that Bob sang traditional Jamaican vendor songs that he had learned while he was living in Kingston. In 1955, Bob learned that his father had died. In the same year, Bob was again separated from Cedella. The meager earnings from the grocery store were not enough to support the two of them. Rural Jamaican life was and is very difficult, and although slavery was abolished in the 1830s, the island still has undertones of slavery. Because she could not support Bob and herself, Cedella opted to take a job as a housekeeper in Kingston. She left Bob on Omeriah's farm and again took the bus to the capital city. This time, instead of searching for her son she was searching for the financial means to properly care for him.

When Bob was aged 11, Omeriah moved Bob to Cedella's older sister's property, about ten miles away from the family farm. Here Bob was in charge of a herd of goats that he had to care for and look after. Lacking any real supervision, Bob and his cousin, Sledger, were constantly in trouble. These troublemaking ways got the pair sent back to Omeriah's farm, and Bob spent the next two years under his grandfather's watchful eye.

In 1957, Cedella had achieved the financial stability to allow for her to call for Bob. However, stability and prosperity are quite different. Bob arrived in Kingston to find that his mother had been living in the city's west-side ghetto. While rural Jamaican life is hard, the west Kingston ghettos were a testament to the underprivileged in the third world. Open sewers, malnourished children, disease, and violence were the characteristics of the place that Bob came to know as Trench Town. Bob and his mother were spared the harshest part of the ghetto, however, and instead lived in the public housing projects called the "government yard."

Jamaica had earlier enjoyed a time of greater prosperity and economic stability. Prior to the sugarcane cutters' strike in 1938, the island's prosperous sugar and banana industries provided a decent living for most of its inhabitants. However, this age of prosperity was forever lost due to the strike. An outgrowth of the strike was the creation of the first Jamaican labor unions, and from the two strongest unions came the two Jamaican political parties. When Jamaica declared independence from Britain on August 6, 1962, these rival parties became locked into a conflict that continues today.

The two parties are the Jamaican Labour Party (JLP) and the People's National Party (PNP), and since the early 1960s each election year has been marked by violence between the two sides. The two parties are completely opposed in membership and mission. The JLP was founded by the right-wing labor organizer Alexander Bustamante, who went on to become Jamaica's first prime minister. Bustamante's party represented the white British and Anglo-Jamaican colonial class, the mercantile middle class composed of Chinese and Lebanese businessmen and storeowners, and the elite black Jamaicans who worked for them. The PNP represented the rest of the island's population, that is, the rural and urban underclass. The PNP was begun by Norman Washington Manley, who also went on to become a Jamaican prime minister.

After Bob arrived in Kingston, he and his mother moved several times, finally settling in an apartment at 19 Second Street. While Cedella was at work in the houses of Kingston's wealthy, Bob attended several schools including Ebenezer, Wesley, and St. Aloysius. Although Bob remained a strong student, he lost interest in school and stopped attending by the time he was 14. He then spent his days playing soccer, hanging out with his friends in the ghetto, and getting into trouble. He also began to get interested in music. Another family that lived in his tenement yard had a son named Neville O'Riley Livingston (b. 1947), who went by the name Bunny. Together, Bob and Bunny began singing cover versions of songs that they had learned on the radio and eventually even fashioned make-shift instruments out of found materials. Their prized possession was a guitar made of copper wire, a sardine can, and a piece of bamboo.

An offshoot of Jamaica's independence was the country's collective search for a new national identity. This search created an environment in which a true Jamaican sound emerged. Until this time, Jamaican music had consisted of mento (a ragged Jamaican calypso) and the American rhythm and blues that was broadcast from Louisiana and Florida. The development of a uniquely Jamaican sound happened fast and took several forms. The first style that developed was called ska. This style has a fast beat, shuffling rhythms, and a combination of elements from mento and rhythm and blues. Ska also had an associated dance, which was a sort of charade in which the dancers acted out everyday domestic chores such as cleaning. Although ska was soon replaced by rock steady, which was a slower, more electric instrument driven style, it did not disappear. In fact, there have been several ska revivals. Ska's second wave flourished in the United States and the United Kingdom in the late 1970s and the 1980s and featured bands such as the English Beat, Madness, the Selector, and the Specials. The mid-1990s saw the rise of ska's third wave, with bands like Less than Jake, the Urge, Sublime, No Doubt, and Reel Big Fish.

At the dawning of the ska era, Bob and Bunny were most interested in the American rhythm and blues sound. Bob particularly liked Fats Domino, Huey "Piano" Smith, and Earl King. He was also influenced by Louis Jordan's jump band style and the close vocal harmonies of the Drifters and the Impressions. Curtis Mayfield, the leader of the Impressions, had a special influence on Bob. While Bob rarely covered other people's songs, he actually incorporated Mayfield's song "People Get Ready" into his own song "One Love." Once Bob embraced the singing style of the Drifters and the Impressions, he knew that he wanted to form a singing group and take a run at music stardom.

While Bob dreamed of becoming a famous singer, Cedella worried about her high school dropout son. She managed to help Bob get a job in a welding shop where he could learn a trade that could support him. While Bob never became a welder, the connections that he made in the welding shop altered the course of his life. One of the other welders was a budding musician named Desmond Dekker. Dekker led the already modestly successful singing group the Aces and he was connected to the Jamaican recording industry. In fact, by the end of the 1960s, Dekker's group had an international hit with the song "Israelites."

GREW UP WAILING

Bob followed his mother's wishes and worked in the welder's shop for a time, because he knew that in order to become a good singer he needed training. He needed to learn the rudiments of how to sing properly and the theory behind the construction of music. The man that was able to provide him with both of those skills lived just around the corner from Bob and Bunny's Second Street yard. Joe Higgs (1940–1999) was half of the successful pre-ska singing duo Higgs and Wilson. He had had success in the early 1960s and was a well-respected member of the Jamaican music scene. However, unlike other successful artists from the ghetto, Higgs choose not to move out of Trench Town. Instead, he converted his Second Street yard into an impromptu music school where aspiring singers were welcome to participate in singing classes. Higgs had perfect pitch and was an expert at singing in close harmony so he was a perfect match for Bob's desires. More importantly, Higgs conducted his classes for free and took all comers.

Bob, Bunny, and Peter

Bob and Bunny began frequenting Higgs's yard and soon were learning how to sing in harmony with each other. Higgs also introduced the pair to a tall, slightly older ghetto youth named Peter MacIntosh, who would soon go by the name Peter Tosh (1944–1987). On Higgs's suggestion, Peter joined Bob and Bunny, making the group a trio. Also, Peter had the distinction of being the only ghetto youth in Higgs's yard to have a factory-made guitar, which he soon taught Bob how to play. Together, the trio formed a singing group called the Teenagers. The group also included two female singers, Beverly Kelso and Cherry Smith, and soon added a fourth male singer in the form of Junior Braithwaite. The group worked well together to create vocal harmony as each singer's voice was in a different range. Bob sang tenor, Bunny sang in a natural-sounding high falsetto, and Peter sang bass. The group did covers of those who had influenced them, including Sam Cooke, Ray Charles, and the Impressions.

Along with their singing tutelage, Higgs also taught Bob how to construct a song. Bob learned that there were three main song sections, the verse (where the story of the song unfolded), the chorus (a section that repeated the song's most catchy material), and the bridge (often composed of a guitar solo). These sections worked in a specific order in the construction of a popular song. The verses and the chorus alternated until about two-thirds of the way through the song, when the bridge was inserted. After the bridge, there were typically repetitions of the chorus material until the song ended. This is the standard verse/chorus song form that was as popular then as it is now.

In 1961, Bob began writing his own songs and the next natural step was to try to get them recorded. Deciding to try to be a solo singer, Bob approached Leslie Kong (1933–1971), who was a Chinese-Jamaican studio owner and who refused to record the Teenagers. The Jamaican recording industry was in its infancy in the early 1960s. There were only a few studios and the studio owners did not want to waste money on a recording that was not a guaranteed moneymaker. Also, the three main studios had immediately cornered the market in Jamaican recording, so together Ken Khouri (Federal Studios), Duke Reid (Treasure Isle Studios), and Clement "Coxsone" Dodd (Studio One) were already governing the style of Jamaican popular music. Having been turned away by Kong, Bob enlisted the help of his welding shop coworker Desmond Dekker. Dekker already had an in at the studios and scored a hit for Kong's Beverley's label with his song "Honour Your Mother and Father." Dekker took Bob back to Kong and he auditioned again. This time, Bob sang for Kong's most recent sensation, the 14-year-old singer Jimmy Cliff. Cliff was sufficiently impressed by Bob's singing to persuade Kong to record a few of Bob's songs.

Solo Singles

Bob recorded "Judge Not," "One Cup of Coffee," and "Terror" in 1962 on Kong's Beverley's label. Kong released these songs as 45-rpm singles, but without any marketing or radio play the singles were not successful. At 16, Bob was a Jamaican recording artist, although not a successful one. At the time of the release, it was assumed that the three songs were all originals written by Bob. However, Christopher Farley has subsequently discovered that "One Cup of Coffee" was actually a cover of a song by Claude Gray, an American singer/songwriter.

One aspect of the Jamaican music scene in the 1960s was the rise of the talent contest. Like the modern Battle of the Bands, various Jamaican businesses sponsored talent contests to try to find the next big hit. Bob sang in several of these contests in the early 1960s and had a modest amount of success. Even as his career was beginning to take off, however, Bob's personal life was difficult. Bob's mother and Bunny's father had an affair that yielded a baby girl whom they called Pearl. Because this created an even more difficult monetary situation, Cedella decided to marry a more stable man. In late 1962, Cedella married Edward Booker, who was already established in a small Jamaican community in Wilmington, Delaware. Cedella and Pearl relocated to Delaware with Booker, and Bob stayed in Jamaica. Cedella did not have enough money for all of them to go; however, she did get Bob a passport and it was at this time that his first and middle names were reversed. Now homeless, 18-year-old Bob was squatting in various spots around Trench Town. By early 1963, Bob was living in the corner of a kitchen on First Street with his friend Vincent "Tartar" Ford. Poor and destitute, Bob and Tartar often sang to keep their minds off of being hungry. Quickly running out of options, Bob rejoined the other members of the Teenagers and abandoned all hope of being a solo singer.

Another music tutor entered the picture when the Rastafarian hand drummer Alvin "Seeco" Patterson began teaching the Teenagers the intricacies of musical rhythm. Patterson was already a professional musician and had deep connections to the Jamaican music industry. In the summer of 1963, Patterson took the Teenagers to audition for Clement "Coxsone" Dodd, the owner of one of the best studios on the island. Dodd's studio was called the Jamaican Recording and Publishing Company Limited, but everyone in Trench Town knew it as Studio One. Patterson had already been talking the band up to Dodd, and the producer knew the sings that Bob had cut for Kong. The group performed one original and three cover songs, but Dodd dismissed them, saying that they needed more practice. Peter, the most aggressive member of the group, told Dodd that they had another song he should hear. The group performed Bob's original composition, "Simmer Down," and Dodd told them that he would record the song. "Simmer Down" was a timely ghetto anthem that warned the youth to control their tempers or the violence in the west Kingston ghetto would only get worse.

For the recording session, the band needed to decide on a name that they could stick with, and they chose the Wailing Wailers based on a passage in the Bible. As was the custom in the Jamaican recording industry, the group was backed by a collection of studio instrumentalists that included some now legendary players such as Ernest Ranglin on guitar, Rico Rodriquez on trombone, Arkland "Drumbago" Parks on drums, and Cluett Johnson on bass. The product of the session was a fast ska version of "Simmer Down" that was dominated by horn lines. All involved were convinced that the song would be a hit. The song was released in time for Christmas 1963 and by early 1964 it had soared to number one on the Jamaican charts. The song sat at the top of the chart for two months and the Wailing Wailers were instant stars.

Chapter 2

OUT OF THE GHETTO, INTO THE LIMELIGHT

With the success of "Simmer Down," the Wailing Wailers became a fixture at Studio One. The recorded regularly and Dodd even allowed Bob to live at the studio. The Wailing Wailers followed up their early success with two more hits n 1964. The songs "It Hurts to Be Alone" and "Lonesome Feeling" were both emotional songs about the pain of loss and loneliness. In 1965, "I'm Still Waiting" was the next Wailing Wailers hit. The song was recorded with the close harmonies of the American doo-wop style. Another Wailing Wailers mainstay was to cover American hits and infuse them with island style. They did this with songs by the Drifters, Aaron Neville, and others. Although the group never got reproduction rights from the original songwriters, they never had legal problems because their covers were never popular outside Jamaica.

FROM SKA TO ROCK STEADY

Living in Dodd's studio gave Bob the opportunity to practice the guitar for hours. It also allowed him to listen to Dodd's rhythm and blues and soul records. Bob immersed himself in the Motown sound and spent hours listening to the products from the soul studios of the American southeast. As Bob was learning American musical style, the Jamaican ska style was giving way to rock steady. In rock steady, the beat speed is less than half as fast as in ska. Also, the ska horn line is gone and is replaced by keyboards. The guitar is emphasizing the second and fourth beat of a four beat measure and the bass is emphasizing beats one and three. The Wailing Wailers adopted this style change and slowed their songs down to accommodate the new style.

In addition to their studio time, the Wailing Wailers spent the mid-1960s playing live. They appeared on Vere John's "Opportunity Hour" and the Ward Theater's "Battle of the Bands." Growing up in the ghetto, Bob had been given the nickname "Tuff Gong" for his no-nonsense street attitude. Bob displayed his temper after losing one of these talent contests to a group called the Uniques. Upon the announcement of the winner, Bob flew into a rage and challenged a member of the winning band to a fight.

An aspect of the new rock steady style was a subset of songs that were associated with the "rude boy" lifestyle. Jamaican rude boys were the ghetto youth who survived on their wits and were often prone to short tempers and violence. Bob often injected that rude boy swagger into his songs. Additionally, rude boy rock steady allowed the bass and drums to dominate the song and did not use the typical ska horns. The Wailing Wailers created a ghetto anthem with their 1965 single "Rude Boy." The song glorified the rude boy attitude and its lyrics were filled with boasting and rude boy slang. Again, Bob and the group had a big hit. Even with this original music success, the Wailing Wailers continued to cover other artists' songs with Tom Jones's "What's New Pussycat" and the Beatles' "And I Love Her." It was also at this time that Bob began the practice, which lasted the rest of his life, of inserting Biblical quotations or paraphrases into his songs.

The end of 1965 also marked the end of the Wailing Wailers. Junior Braithwaite left the group to move to Chicago and Kelso and Smith also departed for greener pastures. Reduced to the core three members, the Wailing Wailers also shortened their name to just the Wailers. This alteration of the group size foreshadowed the constantly changing lineup that marked the entire existence of the Wailers band.

In early 1965, Bob met the female singer Rita Anderson (b. 1950). Rita was the head of a female vocal trio called the Soulettes. She was also a Sunday school teacher, church singer, and respected member of the ghetto community. Like Bob, Rita also gained access to Studio One and aspired to be a recording artist. Rita convinced Bob and Peter to arrange for an audition for her group. Dodd liked what he heard, but in his shrewd business manner told the girls that they needed more work. He brought them in on probation and made Bob their singing coach and manager.

At first, Bob was very strict with the girls and they were scared of him. Soon, though, Bob softened and even admitted that he was attracted to Rita. Bob expressed his feeling for Rita by writing her love notes that he asked Bunny to deliver for him. The pair soon grew closer and the resulting love affair lasted the rest of Bob's short life. At the same time, Bob tired of living in Dodd's studio. Seeing no other solution, Rita took Bob in to live with her, her infant daughter Sharon, and her aunt and uncle. However, her aunt and uncle were not agreeable to the situation and threw the pair out. Cooler heads soon prevailed; a small shack was built behind Rita's aunt and uncle's house, and Bob, Rita, and Sharon all lived there. Bob spent the rest of 1965 working for Dodd, getting closer to Rita and Sharon, and trying to advance his fledgling music career. At the end of the year, the Wailers learned their first important lesson about the record industry. When they went to collect your annual royalties for their record sales from Dodd, they were put off and told that their living allowance was their royalties. A fight ensued and Dodd finally relented, giving the three singers £60 to split. With this, Bob's distrust of record producers began; it continued to grow worse for the rest of his life.

Bob planned a moneymaking trip to Delaware for early 1966. However, he laid down one condition; before he left he wanted to marry Rita. On February 10, 1966, Bob and Rita were married. Friends of the pair heralded the wedding as the union of the two most promising singing groups on the island. Just has his father had done, Bob left Rita the day after the wedding to find work in the United States.

BOB AND RASTAFARIANISM

Bob's stay in Delaware lasted for seven months. During this time, Bob worked a variety of menial jobs. He was a laboratory assistant for the Du Pont Chemical Company and he had part-time jobs as a parking lot attendant, fork lift driver, and dishwasher. The rest of Bob's time was spent writing new songs. He did not particularly care for the fast pace or the climate in Delaware and looked forward to returning to Jamaica and Rita. Also while in Delaware, Bob began his conversion from Catholicism to belief in Rastafarianism. His mother was appalled by the change, but was powerless but to watch as Bob's hair grew into dreadlocks and as he talked ever increasingly about Haile Selassie and Ethiopia.

The wearing of dreadlocks is one aspect of the beliefs of Rastafarian adherents. Sporting these uncombed locks of hair has not been universally adopted by members of the group, but Rastas find precedents for this habit in passages from the Bible. Rastas believe dreadlocks to be supported by Leviticus 21:5 ("They shall not make baldness upon their head, neither shall they shave off the corner of their beard, nor make any cuttings in the flesh") and the Nazarite vow in Numbers 6:5 ("All the days of the vow of his separation there shall no razor come upon his head: until the days be fulfilled, in which he separateth himself unto the LORD, he shall be holy, and shall let the locks of the hair of his head grow"). One reason this hairstyle was adopted was to contrast the kinky hair of black men with the straighter hair of whites. This visible separation was also a part of the American civil rights movement when black Americans worked their hair into large Afros.

Rastafarianism is one of the many syncretic religions found in the Caribbean; others include Santeria in Cuba and Voodoo in Haiti. Religious syncretism is the combining of two disparate religious beliefs, in this case the combining of Catholicism and elements of various African religions. The Rastafarians, and ultimately the Marley family, believed the then emperor of Ethiopia, Haile Selassie I (his name is translated as "Power of the Trinity"), was in fact a reincarnation of Jesus sent to earth to rescue them from their oppression. Haile Selassie was baptized Tafari Makonen and was given the title/rank of *ras*, which loosely translates to duke or head. He was a descendent of an old bloodline that traced its origins back to Menelik, who was the first son of Solomon and Makeba the Queen of Sheba. He was believed to be the 225th descendant of this bloodline and was variously referred to as Neguse Negest (King of Kings), Lord of Lords, Conquering Lion of the Tribe of Judah, Elect of God, Light of the Universe, and Emperor of Ethiopia. The pan-Africanist and leader of the Universal Negro Improvement Association, Marcus Garvey, found a basis in the Old Testament for the belief that Haile Selassie was a reincarnation of Jesus and was the one who originally professed Selassie's deification. Selassie did nothing during his life to discredit this notion and perpetuated this belief among Rastas all over the world.

Bob returned from Wilmington in October with plans to jump start his Jamaican recording career. The Jamaica to which he returned was dramatically changed from the one he had left less than a year earlier. In his absence, Haile Selassie I had visited the island and this visit was heralded by many as the coming of the Redeemer. Even Rita went to view Selassie as he passed by in a motorcade. Upon his return, Rita told Bob that she had seen the marks left on Selassie's hands from being hung on the cross, the stigmata.

In addition to the Rastafarian fever gripping Jamaica's underclass, the music of the island had also changed. While Bob was in Delaware, the Soulettes had scored a hit with their Studio One release "Pied Piper" and the Wailers had continued to perform. The group had success with the singles "Who Feels It," "Dancing Shoes," "Rock Sweet Rock," "The Toughest," "Let Him Go," "Dreamland," and others.

On Bob's return, the Wailers were also the first Jamaican group to outwardly adopt the look of adherents of Rastafarianism. Bob's hair was already starting to knot into locks, and Peter had stopped shaving and cutting his hair; Bunny had been interested in Rastafarian beliefs earlier than the other two. Additionally, the group began following other tenets of Rastafarianism. They adopted the strict Ital diet, and engaged in active Bible reading and aggressive ganja smoking. Rasta sentiments also began appearing in their music with Haile Selassie themed songs and Rasta philosophy injected into lyrics.

The Rastafarian use of ganja (marijuana) has been a point of contention with the Western world since Rastafarianism began. Rastas do not smoke ganja for the high; the drug is as illegal in Jamaica as it is in the United States and smoking ganja has led to many Rastas being jailed. Instead, Rastas consider ganja the "wisdom weed" of Rastafarianism and smoke it to gain wisdom. It became part of their religious rites (rituals) as a means for bringing oneself closer to Jah (God). Rastas found a basis for the use of ganja in the Bible. Psalm 104:14 stated: "He causeth the grass to grow for the cattle and herb for the service of man." Smoking ganja became a sacrament of Rastafarianism. It was used at their religious meetings, called grounations, and has been described as the "healing of the [African] nation." Further, Rastas have a ceremonial approach to smoking ganja through the use of a "chalice" (a rudimentary water pipe that cools and filters the smoke). Ganja is not the only herb used in Rastafarianism; there are numerous others used for medicinal and dietary purposes.

Another change that occurred with Bob's return from Delaware was that the Wailers split with Dodd's Studio One. Friction between Bob and Dodd had long been getting worse and the Wailers' Rastafarian ways did not fit with Dodd's image for the studio. Also, the Wailers had released over a hundred singles on the Studio One imprint, five of which had reached the Jamaican top 10. However, they had seen very little money from all of their record sales. Also, Dodd had been selling Wailers singles for reissue in England and making a healthy profit. None of this money was given to the Wailers, and while Dodd was getting rich the Wailers continued to struggle for subsistence.

Bob then replaced Dodd with his new spiritual guide, a Rastafarian elder named Mortimer Planno. Planno did not just aid Bob in understanding the ways of Rastafarianism; he also became the Wailers' manager. As Bob's faith grew, so did his family. Rita was pregnant and Bob decided to move his growing family to the Malcolm family farm in St. Ann. The Marley family stayed in St. Ann until 1970. During this period, Bob only traveled to Kingston to conduct occasional business. The family lived by subsistence farming and soon Rita delivered a baby girl named Cedella. Throughout this period, Bob continued to write songs.

Since the Wailers had split with Dodd, they were in need of a record label. The group opted to form their own label, which they called Wail'N Soul'M. The Wailers released "Selassie Is the Chapel" and "This Man Is Back." For their work in the studio, the Wailers began employing the producer Clancy Eccles (1940–2005). They then released the singles "Nice Time" and "Stir It Up." For a brief period everything went well. However, at the end of 1967, the stamping machine that actually made the Wailers singles broke and the Wail'N Soul'M imprint folded. The group's bad experience with Dodd and the trouble with their recorded stamper foreshadowed the difficulties that they would have for the rest of the band's existence.

The year 1968 did not treat the band much better. Peter was arrested for taking part in a protest against the white supremacist government in Rhodesia, Africa, and Bob and Bunny were each temporarily jailed for marijuana possession. Bob served a month in jail, but Bunny was sentenced to a year because he was caught with a significant quantity of the drug. The group turned this opposition into the material on which they based their songs, making a positive out of a negative situation. Also, the Marley family ended the year on a high note when Rita gave birth to a son that they named David. Although he was named David Marley, he quickly earned the nickname Ziggy and that is how he is known to the world today.

The end of the 1960s was a tumultuous time for Bob and the Wailers. The group paid careful attention to the civil rights movement in the United States and identified with the statements made by Martin Luther King, Jr. They also deepened their faith in Rastafarianism. Planno took Bob to visit a Rasta enclave in Jones Town where he learned of a group of Rastas who held themselves to an even stricter doctrine and set of practices. The members of the group called themselves the Twelve Tribes of Israel and spent long hours in grounations that were filled with praying, drumming, chanting, and smoking ganja. Bob gradually became closely associated with the Twelve Tribes. Because he was born in February, Bob became part of the tribe of Joseph. Through the Twelve Tribes, Bob met the African American pop singer Johnny Nash. Nash had an international hit with this song "I Can See Clearly Now," and through his connections, Nash helped the Wailers reach a larger audience.

Nash and his business partner, Danny Sims, began operating a record label in 1964. The original label, called JoDa, was unsuccessful. However, with their growing connections in the Caribbean, Nash and Sims opened the Cayman Music label. The label was based in the Cayman Islands and due to the relative cheapness of making recordings in the Caribbean, Nash and Sims's new company prospered. The pair also realized that they could make significant money exporting Jamaican music to the rest of the world. Bob and the Wailers auditioned for Nash and Sims and a recording agreement was reached. However, the group could not go directly into the studio because Bunny was still in jail.

The Wailers were excited about the prospect of working with Nash and Sims, as the pair wanted to promote the band on an international level. With the negotiating help of Planno, the Wailers and Cayman Music entered into an agreement in which the band members were hired as song writers for the label. With Bunny's release from prison in September of 1968, the group began recording for Cayman Music and over the next four years cut more than eighty singles.

In early 1969, Sims launched the JAD Records label and used it to record more early Wailers singles, such as "Mellow Mood," "Put It On," "How Many Times," and "There She Goes." These songs all fell into the rock steady style and did not display the Rastafarian lyrics that the group would become known for. Early 1969 brought another change to the Jamaican popular music style. The rock steady beat slowed down even further and rock steady became reggae. The group Toots and the Maytals ushered in the new sound with the song "Do the Reggay," and soon the sound swept the island. Coincidentally, as the sound that the Wailers would become famous for was starting to gel, the band was being given greater freedom from the constraints of their Cayman and JAD contracts.

With their freedom from Cayman and JAD, Bob and the Wailers returned to the studio of Bob's first producer, Leslie Kong. With Kong, the Wailers recorded enough material for an album. The Wailers used Kong because he was recognized as one of the hottest producers on the inland at the time and he was also fostering the new reggae sound. The newly recorded songs included "Soul Shakedown Party," "Stop That Train," "Caution," "Go Tell It on the Mountain," "Soon Come," "Can't You See," "Soul Captive" "Cheer Up" "Back Out," and "Do It Twice." Kong then issued these songs as singles in Jamaica and England, but none of them was commercially successful. Kong then informed the group that he planned to release the material as an album called *The Best of the Wailers*. This news sent the Wailers into a rage as they all believed that their best material was yet to come. Against the group's protests, the album was released. However, before Kong could reap any benefits, he died of a massive heart attack at age 38.

LEE "SCRATCH" PERRY

Again disillusioned by the Jamaican record industry, Bob planned another trip to Delaware to make enough money to launch his own record label and thereby retain control over the Wailers' music. In the spring of 1969, Bob again went to live with his mother. This time Bob worked at a Chrysler automobile plant in addition to holding down several other jobs. When he returned to Jamaica several months later, the money that he had made went to supporting his family. Nevertheless, Bob was ready to return to the studio and took the Wailers back to Studio One to work for Clement "Coxsone" Dodd. The second series of recordings with Dodd was even better than the first, as Dodd had employed a new sound engineer, Lee "Scratch" Perry (b. 1936).

The union of the Wailers and Perry proved to be a good one and together they produced a unique sound. The production was rougher than it had been with Kong, Bob's vocals were left raw, and the bass and the drum were the lead instruments. The guitar played offbeat chocked-chord chops and the sounds was more reminiscent of the Wailers' rude boy days. The backing band was Perry's studio group called the Upsetters (the Upsetter was another of Perry's nicknames). Two members of this band ended up playing with Bob until he died. The Barrett brothers, Aston ("Family Man") on bass, and Carlton ("Carlie") on drums, became the rhythm section for the Wailers.

In late 1969 and early 1970, the Barrett brothers, Perry, and the Wailers worked in the studio to create the classics "Duppy Conqueror" and "Mr. Brown." Both songs were released as singles with their own dub versions on the B-sides. The Jamaican practice of dubbing referred to making a single that had the original song on the A-side and the song without the lyrics on the B-side. This was done so that a DJ at sound system parties could "toast," or supply his own words, over the lyric-less side to whip the crowd into a frenzy and then turn the record over and play the song in the complete version. The sound systems were giant mobile stereos that were used at parties around the island.

At the beginning of the 1970s, the Wailers again launched their own record label. Called Tuff Gong, after Bob's nickname, the new label failed as fast as the Wail'N Soul'M imprint had. Perry, who had separated himself from Dodd and opened his own record shop and label, invited the Wailers to work on his new Upsetter imprint. The material created by the Wailers with Perry was some of the band's best early material, including "Small Axe," "Corner Stone," "Don't Rock My Boat," and "It's Alright." The Wailers/Perry collaboration lasted through the early part of the 1970s and yielded over a hundred tracks. Mature Wailers/Perry material reflected the group's Rastafarian interests with songs such as "Lively Up Yourself," "Kaya," and "400 Years." "Trench Town Rock" was released in 1971 and again put the Wailers on the Jamaican charts.

In 1971, the Wailers finished their work with Perry. The group was looking for another creative outlet. Bob learned that Nash was going to work on a movie soundtrack in Sweden and Nash asked Bob to come with him. On the way, Bob dropped Rita and the children off at his mother's, and Rita found work as a nurse in a Delaware hospital.

After Bob and Nash's work on the Swedish film score was complete, the pair traveled to London, where Nash was trying to broker a recording contract with the CBS. When the deal was struck, Bob brought the rest of the Wailers to London, where he believed that Sims was working a similar deal for the Wailers. The Wailers recorded in the CBS studios, where they worked as Nash's backing band. While a separate deal did not materialize for the Wailers, they did get more recording experience and returned to Jamaica with high hopes for future English success.

Back in Jamaica, the Wailers recorded at Harry J's studio and Dynamic Sounds. For Harry J's owner Harry Johnson, the Wailers recorded at a vigorous pace for four months. At this time, the Wailers included Bob, Peter, and Bunny plus the Barrett brothers and a 15-year-old keyboard player named Tyrone Downie. An unofficial member of the band was added in the form of Alan "Skill" Cole. Cole was one of Jamaica's most talented soccer players and he was a great fit as Bob's trainer and confidant.

The success of "Trench Town Rock" created a great demand for the Wailers around the island. It also marked the end to songwriting that was not of substance. Also, for the first time the Wailers made significant money from one of their hits. With Bob's share, Bob and Rita established Tuff Gong Records, a record shop where they sold Wailers releases. In addition to the money from "Trench Town Rock," Perry was still releasing Wailers singles and cutting the band in on the profits. Bob again reinvested his share and opened Tuff Gong Productions, which was meant to keep up with the demand for Wailers material. There followed another period of productivity that produced songs such as "Satisfy My Soul," "Mr. Chatterbox," "Natural Mystic," "Concrete Jungle," and "Reggae on Broadway."

While Bob was busy making records and running the production company, he was kept in balance by Cole who had him on a schedule of exercise that included a great deal of soccer playing and physical activity. Bob was also a full-fledged Rastafarian and ate only according to the Ital diet. Ital was the Rasta diet of organic foods, no meat other than fish, no salt, and no alcohol. During this period of extreme activity, the bond of the original three Wailers, Bob, Peter, and Bunny, started to fray.

It was also at this time that Bob began his long and tumultuous relationship with the Jamaican political scene. He did this by giving the Wailers' backing to the People's National Party (PNP). At this time, the PNP was led by Michael Manley, who had been working to create alliances with the underclass and the Rastafarians. Manley was the one who brought Haile Selassie I to Jamaica and some of Manley's popularity with the Rastas came from his relationship with the Ethiopian ruler. As a show of support, Bob and Rita rode on the PNP Musical Bandwagon, on which they played and sang songs. This showed everyone on the parade route that the Wailers were supporting the PNP in the 1972 general election.

ISLAND RECORDS AND CHRIS BLACKWELL

In the fall of 1971, Bob and the Wailers returned to England to continue the pursuit of a CBS contact for the Wailers. With Nash's help, Bob and the Wailers launched a three-week CBS-sponsored tour. The tour was successful, but did not lead to record sales for the Whalers. Matters were complicated when Nash and Sims disappeared unexpectedly. This left the Wailers stranded in England with no income or plans. In the face of this bad situation, Bob took matters into his own hands and went to meet with the head of the London-based Island Records Company, Christopher Blackwell. Blackwell already had a solid roster of talent including Steve Winwood's group Traffic, Cat Stevens, Free, King Crimson, and Jethro Tull. Although Blackwell specialized in rock and roll bands, he had a deep interest in the Caribbean music scene and he was already aware of the Wailers' music.

In the wake of Bob and Blackwell's meeting, the record producer fronted the band £8,000 sterling, which was enough money to get back to Jamaica and return to the studio. Blackwell's deal with the Wailers was that they would produce a full-length reggae album in exchange for the money. Rita and the children returned from Delaware and with everyone back in Jamaica, the Wailers went back into the studio.

CATCH A FIRE

The 1972 recording session yielded the *Catch a Fire* album. "Catch a Fire" was Jamaican slang for someone getting in trouble or "catching hell." The album was recorded at Dynamic Sound, Harry J's, and Randy's studios. The result was a collection of nine songs including "Concrete

Jungle," "Slave Driver," "400 Years," "Stop That Train," "Baby We've Got a Date," "Stir It Up," "Kinky Reggae," "No More Trouble," and "Midnight Ravers." The album itself was groundbreaking in format. Up to this time, reggae songs had been released as singles with an A and B side. With *Catch a Fire*, the format changed to the long-playing record, which allowed greater cohesion in the release of blocks of songs.

The original pressing of the album reflected the Wailers' creative spirit. The first vinyl edition of the album depicted a large stainless steel Zippo light with the title engraved on it. The album jacket was hinged on the left-hand side and revealed a cardboard cutout of the trademarked Zippo lighter windproof mechanism with a flame shooting out of its top. Illustrative of the album's title, these flames also foreshadowed the Wailers' rise to international stardom. The Zippo lighter jacket was unique, but also expensive to produce. As a result, the Zippo lighter edition was held to only 20,000 units. Subsequent pressings of the album were released with a traditional package that displayed a large picture of Bob taking a hit off a large cone-shaped spliff (Jamaican slang for a marijuana cigarette).

For this album, the Wailers were Bob, Peter, Bunny, Aston and Carlie Barrett, and a variety of Jamaican studio instrumentalists. Additional vocals were added by Rita and her friends Judy Mowatt and Marcia Griffiths. The collection of three female backup singers would later become known as the I-Threes. With the basic recording done, Bob took the master tapes to London for mixing and overdubbing. At Blackwell's request, rock and roll style overdubs were added by guitarist Wayne Perkins (who was famous for his work at Muscle Shoals studios) and keyboard player John "Rabbit" Bundrick (who was also well known for his work with Johnny Nash and the rock bands Free and The Who). Overdubbing is the process of adding new tracks to an already "complete" recording. With Perkins and Bundrick's overdubs, the record took on a more mainstream rock sound, which Blackwell thought would allow it to reach a larger audience. Blackwell's instincts were correct and although it was not a big commercial success, *Catch a Fire* brought the Wailers to the mainstream and changed the way that reggae music was made and marketed.

Also in 1972, Rita gave birth to another son, whom the Marleys called Stephen. With this new addition, the family moved out of Kingston to a small house in Bull Bay, east of the city. This move signaled a change for the Marley family; they had made it out of the ghetto and would never live there again. Significantly, Bob often preferred to stay in Kingston, at Blackwell's house at 56 Hope Road, instead of returning to Bull Bay with Rita and the children each night. This time spent apart from Rita afforded Bob the opportunity to begin his string of extramarital affairs. Through his adult life, Bob fathered children with several women other than Rita, though the couple remained married until Bob's death. In the early 1970s, Bob fathered children with Patricia Williams (a son named Robbie), Janet Hunt (a son named Rohan), and Janet Bowen (a daughter named Karen). The year 1972 also saw the election of Michael Manley as the prime minister of Jamaica and with him came hopes for a brighter future for the Jamaican underclass.

Part of Bob's deal with Blackwell was that the Wailers retained all the Caribbean rights to their recordings. This left Bob free to issue singles from *Catch a Fire* on the island through his Tuff Gong record shop. Although his success was still modest compared to what it would be by the end of the decade, Bob was now recognized everywhere he went on the island. Further, with the release of *Catch a Fire*, it dawned on the Wailers that they were now professional musicians who would no longer have to work other jobs to make a living. In the wake of their first full-length album, the Wailers prepared to mount a tour of England and the United States. For this, they needed a full-time keyboard player, as Downie was still too young to travel with the band. The group found its new keyboard player in the Now Generation band with the successful recruitment of Earl "Wya" Lindo.

CATCH A FIRE TOUR

The *Catch a Fire* tour began in April 1973 with the group's arrival in London. Amazingly, the Wailers found another release credited to them for sale. The *African Herbsman* album was a collection of several of the group's more popular songs that had been recorded for Lee "Scratch" Perry. Perry had licensed the material to Lee Goptal, who had subsequently released the album without the approval of the band. The record included the songs "Lively Up Yourself," "Small Axe," "Duppy Conqueror," "Trench Town Rock," "African Herbsman," "Keep On Moving," "Fussing and Fighting," "Stand Alone," "All in One" (a medley of "Bend Down Low," "Nice Time," "One Love," "Simmer Down," "It Hurts to be Alone," "Lonesome Feeling," "Love and Affection," "Put It On," and "Duppy Conqueror"), "Don't Rock My Boat," "Put It On," "Sun Is Shining," "Kaya," "Riding High," "Brain Washing," and "400 Years." Although the release of this album was not sanctioned by the Wailers, it did help to maintain interest in the band in between its first and second Island Records releases. While in England, the Wailers played 19 shows at clubs and universities.

The Wailers returned to London at the end of the tour and while there, they made appearances on the BBC programs *The Old Grey Whistle Test* and *Top Gear*. Elated by their newfound exposure, the Wailers returned to Jamaica for some much-needed rest. A problem had developed during the English leg of the Wailers' tour, as Bunny suffered while touring due to his strict adherence to the Ital diet. Thus, when the Wailers returned to Jamaica, Bunny informed Bob that he would not be joining the band for the North American leg of the tour. Bob consulted with Peter and together they decided to recruit Joe Higgs, their old singing instructor, to replace Bunny for the tour. Another difficulty that the Wailers faced was that they needed a full-time manager to run the now busy band's schedule. Blackwell hired Lee Jaffe to fill this role and Jaffe set off for the United States to book shows for the upcoming tour. The American leg of the tour featured a long stand at Paul's Mall in Boston, Massachusetts, followed by a move to New York. The New York shows were all booked at Max's Kansas City, and the Wailers played a week of gigs as the opener for Bruce Springsteen.

BURNIN'

By 1973, the Bob Marley and the Wailers had a successful album out with a major label and had mounted a tour of England and North America. However, they still had not achieved the type of mainstream commercial success that Bob was convinced that they were capable of. The next step toward that success was taken with the November 1973 release of the band's second Island release, *Burnin'*. This release was less heavily modified by Blackwell and reflected the Wailers' interests in Rastafarianism and Jamaican politics.

The cover of the album was a silhouette of the six core Wailers' heads burned into the side of a wooden box. The picture included Bob, Peter, Bunny, the Barrett brothers, and Lindo, and the back of the record jacket had a large picture of Bob taking a drag off a large spliff. The tracks for this album were recorded at Harry J's in Kingston and mixed at the Island Records studios in London. The only musician on the album who was not pictured on the record's cover was the hand drummer Alvin "Seeco" Patterson.

The album consisted of 10 tracks that included "Get Up, Stand Up," "Hallelujah Time," "I Shot the Sheriff," "Burnin' and Lootin'," "Put It On," "Small Axe," "Pass It On," "Duppy Conqueror," "One Foundation," and "Rasta Man Chant." This list represented some old and some new material. Additionally, Bob, Peter, and Bunny each contributed songs that they had written separately. The album as a unit was a call to action to the Jamaican underclass. The Wailers were warning the ghetto dwellers that they needed to take charge of their own destiny instead of leaving it in the hands of those who did not have their best interests at heart.

BURNIN' TOUR

After the album was released, the Wailers again mounted a tour to support it. In an attempt to boost the disappointing sales of this release in the United States, Bob and the Wailers joined the in-progress Sly and the Family Stone tour of the country. Higgs again replaced Bunny, as he had vowed not to tour after his experience on the *Catch a Fire* tour. This tour was a lucky break for the group, as Sly and the Family Stone were already a popular band in America and they were touring after their successful *Fresh* release. Unfortunately, the Wailers were fired from the tour after just four shows. The reasons for the firing were twofold. First, the Wailers were reportedly outplaying the headliners, and the Sly and the Family Stone crowd were not accepting of the Wailers' style of music. The firing again left the Wailers stranded in a strange place.

This time, the group was stuck in Las Vegas and needed to find a way to California to make a scheduled appearance on KSAN-FM. They did manage to get to San Francisco and make their appearance, being met by an enthusiastic audience that they had attracted on their previous tour. Audiences on the California coast maintained a special affinity for Bob and the Wailers throughout the existence of the band. The KSAN broadcast was presented from the Record Plant in Sausalito and comprised a rousing set of songs. The broadcast began with Bob, Peter, and Higgs performing "Rasta Man Chant" acoustically with just traditional Rastafarian hand drums as accompaniment. They then went into full band versions of a series of songs from the first two Island albums.

The end of 1973 found the Wailers back in Jamaica preparing to embark on the English leg of the *Burnin'* tour. This time Higgs also stayed in Jamaica, which left Bob and Peter to front the band. The reduced-strength Wailers played to small crowds who were not excited about the performances. The group played 11 shows in England, appearing at clubs and universities. The poor reception was made worse when Bob and Peter got into a fist fight and Lindo announced that he was leaving the group to return to the Now Generation band. With this, the Wailers headed in opposite directions, leaving Bob in London to contemplate his next move.

The year 1974 dawned with Bob back in Harry J's studio in Kingston, where he was recording new material with a backing band that consisted only of the Barrett brothers and a keyboard player named Bernard "Touter" Harvey. The traditional tight vocal harmonies usually produced by Bob, Peter, and Bunny were now being sung by the female vocal trio, the I-Threes (Rita, Judy, and Marcia.). This relatively stripped down Wailers unit worked on new songs that reflected on Bob's ghetto youth as a means of escaping the troubles of the present.

The group caught a break when they were asked to open for American Motown singing sensation Marvin Gaye when he played a benefit show on the island. The concert was sold out and was an excellent opportunity for the group to feature its new material. At show time, the Wailers band that took the stage again included Bob, Peter, and Bunny, plus the Barrett brothers' rhythm section and Tyrone Downie on keyboards. The Wailers' performance was a big hit and afterward Marvin Gaye's manager, Don Taylor, offered to manage them. Taylor was able to give Bob his most elusive desire, a guarantee of success in the United States, and ultimately Bob agreed to bring Taylor into the fold as the Wailers' manager.

SEARCHING FOR CROSSOVER SUCCESS

Bob was excited about the possibility of crossover success in the United States, but he was dismayed that Peter and Bunny were now obviously planning to leave the Wailers permanently. Peter had long suffered from lack of exposure as Bob was the material front man for the band, and Peter's own more militant sentiments were not being used on the early Wailers records. Bunny also wanted greater freedom to release his own songs, and this, coupled with his refusal to tour, put him at odds with Bob's plans for the band's future.

With the band in a state of crisis, Bob busied himself preparing the next Wailers album. Titled *Natty Dread,* the third Wailers and Island product was the first without Peter and Bunny. The record was a turning point for Bob, as he was finally striking out on his own as the principal songwriter of the band. In addition to Bob, the Barrett brothers, and Touter, the I-Threes provided vocal harmony. Uncredited performers on the album included Lee Jaffe on harmonica, and three horn players named Glen da Costa, David Madden, and Tommy McCook (the horn line of the Zap Pow band).

With Bob now acting as a vocal soloist with a backing band, the new album art reflected his central role. He began the album with his approximation of a Yoruba lookout call that signaled the dawn of the new Wailers band. The Yoruba are a group of people in West Africa that make up about 30 percent of the population of Nigeria, Benin, and Togo. The *Natty*

Dread album cover was an airbrushed picture of Bob alone in the middle of an abstract background of several colors, and the back of the album also depicted Bob only. As was the case with the previous Island Records releases, the recording was done in Jamaica and the mixing was done in London, under Blackwell's careful supervision. An oddity of this album was that it exhibited the Wailers' only use of a drum machine. Drum machine technology only became widely available in the early 1970s and the Wailers' experiment with it indicated their interest in new technology.

While in London for the mixing sessions, Bob and Family Man found the next Wailers' guitarist, Al Anderson. Anderson had been playing in an Afro-rock band called Shakatu. However, he agreed to supply some guitar overdubs on "Lively Up Yourself" and "No Woman, No Cry." After this studio experience, Blackwell offered Anderson the job of guitarist for the Wailers. At first Anderson did not want to give up his position in Shakatu, but he soon realized that the Wailers were going to be a big success. When Anderson agreed to join the Wailers, he became the first non-Jamaican member of the band. As such he had to learn the reggae style from the ground up and spent hours rehearsing with Family Man learning the proper strumming style.

NATTY DREAD

Released in 1974, *Natty Dread* was a collection of old and new songs. The songs on the album were "Lively up Yourself," "No Woman, No Cry," "Them Belly Full (But We Hungry)," "Rebel Music (Three O'Clock Road Block)," "So Jah Seh," "Natty Dread," "Bend Down Low," "Talkin' Blues," and "Revolution." The songs collected for this release exhibit Bob's interests most directly, as they cast Bob as a Rasta preacher who is discussing prophecy and revolution. Additionally, Bob illustrated his Rasta-based distrust of the Catholic Church. On the song "Talkin' Blue," Bob discussed bombing a church, as the Rastas believe that the Pope, and by extension standard Catholicism, are part of the system in place to keep them down. This negative system was described by the Rastas with the Biblical language of Babylon. Thus, when Rasta singers discussed the Babylon system, they were talking about anything that was oppressive to the Rastafarian faithful.

Another feature of Rastafarianism that Bob made great use of was the purposeful misuse of the English language. Bob could speak plain English when he chose to, but he often veiled his meanings by singing in the Jamaican dialect or through the Rastafarian practice of altering language. For example, Rasta believed that Haile Selassie I was Jesus reincarnated

to save them from the Babylon system. The faithful took the Roman nu-
meral I at the end of Selassie's name and reinterpreted it as the capital
letter I. Thus, when Rastas say something about "I and I" they are talking
about themselves and their god. Many of Bob's songs made use of this
"I and I" language as a means of affirming his faith.

Bob's growing militant stance was also evident on *Natty Dread*. The
song "Revolution" was self-explanatory. Simply, Bob was saying that if
the youth were going to create a change in their lives they had to do
it for themselves, and waiting for the government, or anyone else, to do it
for them was a waste of time. "Rebel Music (Three O'Clock Road Block)"
was another of Bob's more incendiary songs. The song was autobiographical and described an incident in which Bob and Family Man got caught
in a road block and knew that their car would be searched due to their
dreadlocks. As the song went, they had to throw away their ganja to avoid
being arrested. Other lyrics in the song included Bob telling the listeners
that they can examine his life because he knows that he is righteous and
faithful to Jah (the word used to refer to the Rastas' God, Haile Selassie).

After the *Natty Dread* release, Bob was interviewed by the Jamaican
daily newspaper. The photographer present at the interview was a UCLA
graduate named Neville Garrick. In the interview, Bob discussed the need
for more touring to support the Wailers records. After the interview, Bob
and Garrick struck up a friendship that resulted in Garrick becoming the
art director for the Wailers.

In the wake of *Natty Dread*, the Wailers began receiving some critical acclaim in the United States. This was the type of support that did
not earn them any money in the short term, but laid the groundwork for
future success. In late 1974, Bob licensed the recording rights of his song
"Slave Driver" to Taj Mahal, an American blues singer who was enjoying
a period of prosperity. Bob also licensed "Guava Jelly" to Barbra Streisand
for her 1974 *Butterfly* album. This did not bring the band much money,
but it certainly increased the level of exposure to its music. The most
important agreement that Bob made that year was granting Eric Clapton
(the British blues guitar genius) the recording rights to the song "I Shot
the Sheriff," which appeared on Clapton's 1974 album, *461 Ocean Bou-
levard*. In Clapton's capable hands, Bob's song went on to be a number
one hit in the United States and soared to number nine in the UK. Bob's
music was played on American and English radio and he gained serious
respect from the rock and roll critics.

As Bob's star continued to rise, any hope for reconciliation with the
original members of the vocal trio faded into the distance. Peter and
Bunny were both working on solo material of their own. Peter was laying

the groundwork for the album that would become the 1976 *Legalize It*, and Bunny was putting together the songs for his 1976 *Blackheart Man* album. Additionally, Peter launched his own Intel-Diplo record label (Intel-Diplo standing for Intelligent Diplomat).

Undaunted, Bob Marley and the Wailers began 1975 with a major gig. The Wailers were asked to open for the Jackson Five when they played a concert in Kingston. This was Bob's first opportunity to really come to the front of the band and display his own personality and charisma. The appearance also featured the debut of Al Anderson on lead guitar and was a huge success. In February 1975, *Natty Dread* was officially released as the third Island/Wailers product and the album received positive feedback from the press in the UK and the United States. With this success, the new and improved Wailers became an international success.

As the Wailers' fame grew, so did Bob's concerns for the management of the band and its increasing revenues. Bob had already worked out a deal with Don Taylor to become the Wailers' manager, but was concerned with Taylor taking a cut of the band's earnings. Bob's bad experiences with music industry insiders had tainted his opinion of Taylor, but he took a chance on the would-be manager. Now Bob also needed to be able to more carefully look after the band's earnings. This job was taken up by Bob's Jamaican lawyer Diane Jobson. The Wailers also needed an operations headquarters. For this, Bob essentially took over Blackwell's house at 56 Hope Road in Kingston. Here the band had rehearsal space and a central location for its headquarters. With the band membership and its supporting forces established, the group prepared to tour in support of *Natty Dread*.

Chapter 3

FROM TOP OF THE ROCK TO
TOP OF THE WORLD

Acting as the Wailers' manager, Taylor arranged a major North American and a brief English tour for the band. For the purposes of this tour, Tyrone Downie was again recruited to work with the group. As Bob was preparing to feature his talents on the world stage, he was also gaining notoriety with regard to his personal life. On February 26, 1976, Bob's eighth child was born. Ky-Mani Marley was the product of Bob's affair with Anita Belnavis, who was a well-known Caribbean table tennis champion. Bob was also cultivating a relationship with the Jamaican beauty queen Cindy Break-speare. This relationship produced another son in 1978, named Damian, and a huge scandal. Bob and Breakspeare's relationship lasted for several years and in the course of this time the beauty queen went on to become Miss World 1976. The media whirlwind that surrounded the couple was largely based on race. The mixture of white and black, and Breakspeare's beauty queen good looks coupled with Bob's ever-lengthening dread-locks, helped to fuel the media circus.

In June 1975, the Wailers embarked on the North American leg of the *Natty Dread* tour. In addition to Bob, the Barrett brothers, Downie, the I-Threes, and Seeco, the Wailers' entourage also included Taylor and Neville Garrick (as artistic and lighting director). A Rasta elder named Mikey Dan also joined the group to provide Ital food, along with Dave Harper (equipment manager) and Tony "Tony G" Garnett (disc jockey and hype man). The huge touring retinue indicated the level of fame that the Wailers had already achieved. They were now touring in style with the type of support that allowed them to exit their hotel room, be chauffeured to the venue, and walk on stage to perform (a sound check was usually required) without any setting up and tearing down.

NATTY DREAD TOUR

During this tour, Bob established his on-again/off-again relationship with the press. Bob's friends and band mates have reported that he very rarely refused an interview, believing that any press publicity was good for the band. However, he also had a reputation as being hard to interview. He was always glad to discuss the band and Rastafarianism, but when questions turned to his personal life, Bob was more evasive. In fact, when questioned on this topic, Bob was known for dropping into such thick Jamaican slang that the interviewer was left wondering what was being discussed.

As the tour progressed, the Wailers' reception grew more enthusiastic. Sold-out shows were frequent; for example, the band played for a crowd of 15,000 at the Schaefer Music Festival, in New York's Central Park. As the band toured the United States and traveled into Canada, the set list for the shows became standard, with "Trench Town Rock," "Burnin' and Lootin'," "Them Belly Full (But We Hungry)," "Road Block," "Lively Up Yourself," "Natty Dread," "No Woman, No Cry," "I Shot the Sheriff," and "Kinky Reggae." Other songs appeared on occasion, such as "I Shot the Sheriff" and "Get Up, Stand Up." At this time, the Wailers gelled into the touring machine that they became known for. Bob was a serious taskmaster when it came to making sure that the group performed well on stage, and mistakes were not tolerated. The appearance of the group also gradually became standard. Bob adopted his characteristic denim jeans and shirt, and by 1975 his dreadlocks stretched down to his shoulders. The I-Threes also began to solidify their standard look, with heads wrapped in red, gold, and green fabric and traditional African dress.

While the tour gave the band greater exposure to the American audience, there were many problems. Taylor's lack of experience showed, as he did not retain a large enough road crew to handle all of the band's equipment. Frequently there were not enough drivers or roadies, and this led to problems with having the instruments ready when the performers arrived. Taylor also treated the band, other than Bob, as employees instead of as talented individuals, which led to several fights.

The Wailers closed the North American leg of the tour with a show at the Roxy Theatre on Sunset Strip in Los Angeles, California. The show was again sold out and in attendance were members of the Rolling Stones in addition to Cat Stevens, Joni Mitchell, Herbie Hancock, George Harrison

and Ringo Starr of the Beatles, and members of the Grateful Dead and the Band. This was an extraordinary display of critical support for the Wailers. The group knew that they had made a solid impression on the American audience and departed for London prepared to conquer another location.

In London, the band played a show at the Hard Rock in Manchester, another at the Odeon in Birmingham, and two at the Lyceum in London. Blackwell attended the first Lyceum show and noticed how enthusiastic the crowd reaction was. He quickly ordered mobile recording equipment so that the show the following night could be recorded. Modern sound engineering technology makes live recording so easy that it is done automatically at each show. However, in 1975, an entire truckload full of recording gear had to be brought to the venue to capture the concert. Blackwell used his industry connections to borrow the Rolling Stones' mobile studio, which the band had ordered built in the late 1960s. It allowed the Rolling Stones to record in remote locations and this movable equipment had been used to record Led Zeppelin, Deep Purple, and the Rolling Stones albums *Sticky Fingers* (1971) and *Exile on Main Street* (1972).

With live sound engineer Dave Harper sitting in the Rolling Stones' mobile recording studio outside the Lyceum Theatre, Bob Marley and the Wailers took the stage on July 18, 1975. The group tore through an abbreviated set list that night after an introduction by Tony Garnett. The recording was a success and captured Bob and the group performing several of their biggest hits. They were rushing the tempos just slightly, and this gave the music an additional sense of urgency. After some further remixing at Island's Basing Street studios, the recording was released under the title *Live!*.

LAST ORIGINAL WAILERS SHOW

An interesting side note with regard to the year 1975 was that during November, Bob, Peter, and Bunny reunited for their last time on stage. American popular musician Stevie Wonder was slated to play a benefit concert at Jamaica's National Stadium. The concert was staged to raise money for the Jamaican Institute for the Blind and Stevie Wonder was well aware of the Wailers' material. The reconstituted Wailers performed at Wonder's benefit concert and he was blown away. Wonder even joined the Wailers on stage for a version of "I Shot the Sheriff." Much has recently been made of the Wailers/Wonder connection and it is worth noting that after their onstage meeting, Wonder wrote a song in tribute to Bob called "Master Blaster." In fact, often when Wonder performed the song, he began with an improvisational chorus, "We're doing it for Bob

Marley." The song goes on to refer to themes in Bob's life such as Jah, music, and unity.

By the end of the summer, the Wailers were back in Jamaica working on more new music. The group then returned to Harry J's studio to begin recording the tracks for their next album. The process was interrupted when on August 27, 1975, Haile Selassie I died at age 83. The death of the Rasta redeemer sent the faithful into a tailspin. Many of the Rasta faithful took Selassie's death as the signal that Rastafarianism itself was flawed. However, others used the death to steel their determination and deepen their beliefs; Bob was in this second group. He called Lee "Scratch" Perry into Harry J's and together the pair created the scorching song "Jah Live."

An interesting circumstance in relation to Selassie's death is that his body was not recovered for formal burial until 1991. Selassie had died from complications following a prostate operation. His doctor disputed the media report that he was responsible for the death of the emperor. There was also speculation at the time that Selassie was assassinated, as there had been repeated attempts to unseat the emperor beginning in the early 1960s. The situation was further confused by the disappearance of the body. This lack of a corpse convinced many Rasta faithful that Selassie had not died. The cry went out in the Rastafarian territories: "You can't kill God." Information surfaced in 1991 revealing that Selassie's remains had in fact been secretly buried at the time of his death. However, with this mystery accompanying Selassie's demise, many Rastas took the circumstances to mean that their religious leader had not died.

The product of Bob and Perry's studio collaboration was the single "Jah Live." The song was as direct a statement of faith as has been uttered for any religion. Here Bob proclaimed that Jah (Haile Selassie) was still alive. He followed this with his sentiments on understanding faith, told through the metaphor of the shepherd. He also criticized all who believed that Selassie had died and professed that not only was he still alive, but that he was powerful enough to scatter his enemies and remain in power.

The final five years of Bob's life were filled with constant activity, creating new songs, releasing seminal albums, and touring in support of his efforts. The Wailers' popularity continually increased, and by the end of the 1970s the group was known in the most remote places in the world. In 1976, Bob kicked off his activity with a full schedule of concerts, interviews, and recording. Bob reached a significant milestone in his blossoming career when he appeared on the cover of *Rolling Stone* magazine and the magazine voted the Wailers the "Band of the Year." Also by 1976, Bob and the Wailers had taken over the house at 56 Hope Road, even though Blackwell was still its official owner.

Early 1976 was spent recording new Wailers' material and trying to get comfortable with fame. Now that the Wailers were international stars, Bob spent long hours in interviews trying to define to the world what it meant to be a Jamaican, a person of mixed race, and a Rastafarian. While Bob was quickly becoming the representative of Trench Town, his hard-won fame did begin to provide him some luxury that his life had lacked. For example, Bob was now making enough money that Cole convinced him to buy a BMW. Generally not interested in the trappings of wealth, Bob was not originally comfortable with this purchase until he noticed that the BMW could stand for Bob Marley and the Wailers, instead of Bavarian Motor Works.

Even with all of the success carrying the Wailers though 1976, there was significant unrest in the band. The instrumentalists were still unhappy with Taylor's treatment of them, and this resulted in Lee Jaffe and Al Anderson leaving the group. To add insult to injury, the pair immediately joined Peter Tosh's band, called Word, Sound, and Power. So, in the middle of the recording sessions for their fifth album, the Wailers were again reduced to Bob and the Barrett brothers. On the heels of these losses, Bob recruited new players for the group. He quickly recruited Earl "Chinna" Smith to serve as rhythm guitarist, and with Blackwell's help the American blues guitarist Don Kinsey joined the Wailers on lead guitar. The album credits for *Rastaman Vibration* reflect the performance of these new additions to the group. However, with the sessions already taking place, Al Anderson was credited with the lead guitar parts on the song "Crazy Bald Head." Also present on the album was Seeco on percussion and Tyrone Downie on keyboards.

RASTAMAN VIBRATION

In the midst of this tumult, Bob Marley and the Wailers issued their fourth Island Records album in May 1976. The album was issued with a drawing of Bob on the front of the record jacket. His dreadlocks had grown down past his shoulders and he was striking a contemplative pose. Also prominently displayed were the Rastafarian colors, red, yellow, black, and green. These colors were derived from the flag of Ethiopia and the significance of the colors was defined within Rastafarianism as black for the people, red for the blood they shed protecting themselves, yellow for the gold stolen from their ancestors, and green for the lost land of Africa. Historically, there have been some disagreements on the meanings of the colors, but their origins in Ethiopia are irrefutable. The background of the album jacket looked like burlap fabric and contained the statement that the album jacket "is great for cleaning herb." The other text was a quote from the Old Testament Blessing of Joseph. Because Bob was allied with the Tribe of Joseph of the Twelve Tribes of Israel Rastafarian sect, this passage professed his strength and generosity.

Rastaman Vibration was the Wailers' biggest success yet. It climbed to number eight on the American pop charts. Bob said of the album that on it he was not as concerned with the music as with the message. The themes of the songs contained on the album range from calls for revolution to discussions of politics. The tracks were "Positive Vibration," "Roots, Rock, Reggae," "Johnny Was," "Cry to Me," "Want More," "Crazy Bald Head," "Who the Cap Fit," "Night Shift," "War," and "Rat Race." Bob's practice of writing autobiographical lyrics was evident on this album. "Night Shift" was about his time working in Delaware and talked about his time spent driving a forklift and pining for Jamaica, his wife, and his children. "Rat Race" was Bob's take on the role of the Rastas and politics. Here Bob warns that Rastas will not be involved in any political maneuvering. The song was written as Jamaica was becoming embroiled in the violence leading up to the election of 1976. Regardless of Bob's antipolitical convictions, the events surrounding the 1976 election forever changed his life.

The most significant Rastafarian song on the album was "War." The lyrics of this song were taken from a speech that Haile Selassie delivered to the United Nations on October 4, 1963. In the speech, Selassie demanded equality for people of all colors regardless of location or faith. Bob's Rastafarian faith, even in the wake of Selassie's death, was also affirmed on the title track, "Rastaman Vibration." Also on the album, Bob made repeated use of quotations from the Bible and biblical paraphrases. This use of Old Testament material became a trademark of Bob's mature lyric writing and illustrated his continued adherence to the Rastafarian faith.

RASTAMAN VIBRATION TOUR

The spring and summer of 1976 brought another Wailers tour. In April, the group launched the *Rastaman Vibration* tour, which was slated to cross North America and Western Europe. The tour was the most extensive to date and exposed an ever-growing audience to the group. The Wailers' touring band was back up to full strength with 10 members including Bob, the Barrett brothers, the I-Threes, Seeco, Downie, Smith, and Kinsey. Added to this were Taylor the manager, Bob's trainer Cole, the cook Tony "Gillie" Gilbert, Garrick the art and lighting director, Garnett the band's hype man and road manager, and Dennis Thompson as soundman.

The tour officially began at the Tower Theater in Upper Darby, Pennsylvania. Bob's mother, Cedella Booker, came to this show and it was the first time that she saw her son perform live in concert. Next the Wailers played in Washington, DC, Massachusetts, and New York. They crossed into Canada for shows in Montreal and Toronto and then returned to the United States to play Buffalo and Cleveland. Next, the group swept through the Midwest before playing Texas and finishing up the U.S. leg with seven shows in California. After a stop in Miami, the group pressed on to Western Europe and played in Germany, Sweden, the Netherlands, France, and Wales. The tour ended with 10 shows in England. On most of these stops, the Wailers played sold-out houses and were now playing to people who already knew the songs.

The show on May 26 at the Roxy Theatre in Hollywood, California, was a particular highlight. The American singer/songwriting legend Bob Dylan was in the audience, and the Wailers played a scorching set. Bob Marley was a self-professed fan of Dylan's song writing, and the reggae superstar treated the folk icon to one of the band's best performances. The concert was recorded and has subsequently been released in a two-CD boxed set. That night the Wailers' set included an enthusiastic introduction by Tony "Tony G" Garnett followed by "Trench Town Rock," "Burnin' and Lootin'," "Them Belly Full," "Rebel Music," "I Shot the Sheriff," "Want More," "No Woman, No Cry," "Lively Up Yourself," "Roots Rock Reggae," and "Rat Race." The band had hit their touring stride and played a wonderfully tight set. Bob spent the evening center stage with this signature Les Paul guitar, dreadlocks flying, and hands often raised defiantly in the air. The I-Threes were to Bob's left in matching black dresses and African head wraps. The show ended with an encore performance of "Positive Vibration" and a medley of "Get Up, Stand Up/No More Trouble/War."

GUN COURT

At the end of the tour, the Wailers returned to Jamaica to rest and refocus their efforts on their next recording. The election lead-up was still coming to a boil and Kingston was in a state of emergency declared by Manley. The Manley government had significantly weakened its standing on the island by making moves that seemed to ally the island with Fidel Castro's Communist government in Cuba. Manley's actions had destabilized Jamaica's already weak economy and led to shortages of some of the island's necessities, such as cooking oil and food staples.

Further, a large quantity of hand guns had mysteriously appeared on the island and were being used to escalate the pre-election violence. In Jamaica, possession of a gun was an especially heinous crime. The Jamaican government had been patterned on the British system when the island achieved independence in 1962. However, on April 2, 1974, Jamaica established the Gun Court. The Gun Court was a combination court and prison established to prosecute and punish anyone committing a crime involving a gun. The court was afforded the power to detain criminals indefinitely and subject them to hard labor. Mandatory sentences were enforced until 1983, when the practices of the Gun Court were ruled unconstitutional. During the Gun Court's decade of unrestricted operation, countless ghetto youths were jailed with no hope of returning to regular society.

Another oddity of the 1976 election was that while Manley was courting Castro, the JLP opposition leader, Edward Seaga, was accused of allying himself with the American CIA. This was apparently done to help him win control of the island, but resulted in further destabilizing Jamaica to the point that the island practically dissolved into civil war in the mid-1970s. Everyone on the island was affected by the two Jamaican political powers wrestling for control. Recognizing the harm that was being done, Bob proposed to stage a concert for Jamaicans, to thank the island's population for their support of the band. Dubbed the "Smile Jamaica" Concert, the event was scheduled to take place on Kingston's National Heroes Park on December 5, 1976. In order to stage such an event, Bob needed the approval of the prime minister's office. This approval was granted, but in an act of pure political maneuvering, the PNP announced the date of the next general election as December 20. In so doing, the PNP created a situation in which it seemed the Bob Marley and the Wailers were backing the reelection of Michael Manley of the PNP.

This sent Bob into a rage, but the concert had already been announced, supporting acts were already booked, and Bob and the Wailers had already recorded the song "Smile Jamaica" with Perry in his Black Ark studios. The concert was meant to defuse the violence on the island and reduce the constant warring between the two parties. Bob was essentially trying to save his ghetto brothers and sisters as the pre-election violence was always hottest in the ghetto. Goon squads recruited by each party frequently clashed on ghetto streets, leading to a great many "civilian" deaths.

ATTEMPTED ASSASSINATION

With the warped perception about the "Smile Jamaica" concert, the violence of the 1976 election came directly to Bob's 56 Hope Road house.

Two days before the concert, Bob and the Wailers were at the house on Hope Road rehearsing for their upcoming performance. The band took a break and one of the I-Threes, Judy Mowatt, asked Bob to have someone take her home. She was pregnant and not feeling well, so Bob asked Garrick to take the BMW and return Judy to her home. As they were pulling out of the driveway at 56 Hope Road, Don Taylor was pulling in to supervise the rehearsal. Bob, Taylor, and Kinsey were relaxing in the kitchen waiting for Blackwell, who was supposed to be coming to meet Taylor.

Unnoticed by Taylor, his car had been followed into the driveway by two others. Six gunmen slipped out of these two cars and opened fire on the house. The kitchen was situated at the rear of the house, up a few stairs. Bob, Taylor, and Kinsey heard the gunfire and immediately saw the barrel of a gun coming though the kitchen door. Everyone dived for cover as the gunman opened fire. Bob ducked for cover by the refrigerator, but Taylor was left relatively exposed in the middle of the room. When the shooting stopped, Taylor had been riddled with bullets; Bob had been shot once and the bullet was lodged in his left forearm; and Rita had been shot once in the head but the bullet did not pierce her skull. A Wailers' associate named Lewis Simpson (or maybe Lewis Griffiths—sources conflict) was badly wounded.

Incredibly, no one was killed. Taylor was shot five times in the midsection and had to be flown to Miami for surgery. Rita and Bob were both taken to the hospital and treated. Rita was treated and released with a bandage around her head. Bob was informed that if the doctors removed the bullet from his arm he could lose feeling in his left hand. Bob refused to take the risk, as he wrote his songs accompanying himself on the guitar, so the bullet was left where it had lodged. Overall, things could have been much worse. The bullets that were spayed into the kitchen had not been accurately aimed. In fact, many of them ricocheted around the room leaving holes in the walls that are still visible today. Eventually, everyone made full recoveries from their wounds over the course of time.

Surprisingly, Jamaican Prime Minister Michael Manley visited Bob while he was being treated at the hospital. Manley placed Bob under the protection of the Jamaican security service and he was taken away from the hospital under armed escort. The prime minister was still planning for a Wailers appearance at the "Smile Jamaica" Concert, so protecting Bob was protecting his own political interests. Once Blackwell heard of the shooting, he made his mansion on Strawberry Hill available to the wounded Wailers. Strawberry Hill is high in Jamaica's interior Blue Mountains. Here Bob spent the night trying to sort out the situation and worrying about the future of his band, all under heavy guard provided by the government and by area Rastas. Bob's mind was heavy with concern for his wounded friends and family; additionally, he needed to decide if the band was still going to play the concert.

December 4, 1976, dawned as Bob was beginning his recovery at Strawberry Hill. His main activity for the day was collecting the Wailers, who had scattered in the wake of the shooting, and deciding whether or not to play the concert the following day. Bob was further put on edge with the news that the would-be killers were still at large. Bob spent the day trying fitfully to make sense out of the shooting. It was agreed that the assassination attempt had been politically motivated, but by what political faction was still a mystery (the details surrounding the event have never been fully explained; the outcome was that Bob was not on the island when the election was held).

Regardless of his remaining doubts, Bob took action. He obtained a set of powerful walkie-talkies from the film crew that Blackwell had hired to film the concert. With these, Bob was able to round up the band and monitor the situation in Kingston as he continued to mull over the safety of playing the concert. Bob quickly learned that the news of the attempted assassination had crossed the island. The supporting bands had all canceled their appearances at the concert and the situation at Heroes Park was precarious. Bob took solace in the fact that his old friend Stephen "Cat" Coore, of the band Third World, was on the scene and that Coore's band had agreed to perform and test the waters.

Soon, enough of the Wailers were found to make a performance possible. Coore informed Bob that there were already in excess of 50,000 people at the venue at 4:00 p.m. Still at Strawberry Hill, Bob remained undecided about performing. His resolve was further tested when Rita arrived with her head still bandaged and told him that they should cancel the concert. Serving his party's own purposes, PNP Housing Minister Anthony Spaulding came on the scene to try to convince Bob to perform. Bob was even more conflicted because the concert had been his own idea. Giving in to negative circumstances was not in Bob's personality, but selflessly giving of his gifts and prosperity was.

THE "SMILE JAMAICA" CONCERT

After much deliberation, Bob made the decision to perform the concert. He, Spaulding, and Rita rode down into the city under heavy guard and arrived at the venue to find 80,000 people waiting for the Wailers. In pure defiance of those who sought to silence his voice, Bob Marley and the Wailers took the stage. Checking to see who else was with him, Bob counted Carlie Barrett his drummer, Tyrone Downie his keyboard player, Cat Coore the guitarist for the Third World band, the horn section from Zap Pow, and five of the hand drummers from the band Ras Michael and the Sons of Negus. Bob began his set with a brief announcement in which he said that when he came up with the idea of the concert there was not supposed to be any politics involved. He and the band then launched into a searing 90-minute set with the anti-oppression song "War."

The Wailers' set was supposed to be short, but Bob was rapt with the spirit of the event and pushed the band to continue. A highlight was the performance of "So Jah Seh," which was likely the only time that the group played this song live. The show continued through the Wailers' set without disturbance. During the Wailers' set, Kinsey came on stage wearing a brown tunic to hide his injuries. Conversely, Bob lifted his shirt to show the audience that the reports of the attempted assassination were true, but that he had not succumbed to his wounds.

After the concert, Blackwell again gave Bob the use of the house at Strawberry Hill. Bob spent the night planning his next move and still grappling with the implications of the attempted assassination. Bob believed that the first move to make to ensure his safety was to leave the island. He and Garrick left Jamaica the next day, heading for the island of Nassau in the Bahamas. Nassau is one several small islands off of the southeastern tip of Florida. The Nassau move was well thought out as Blackwell had already moved his Caribbean base of operations to this island due to the constant upheavals in Jamaica. Also, Blackwell was already working on building the world-class Compass Point Studios on Nassau (the studios opened in 1977 and are still in use with a client list of international stars).

SELF-IMPOSED EXILE

While Bob assumed that Nassau would be a safe haven from the turmoil of Jamaica, the immigration officials on the island were not sure if it was safe for them to have Bob on the island. After much deliberation, Bob and Garrick were given temporary permission to stay in Nassau, with the proviso that they could be forced to leave the island at any time. The pair then settled in at Blackwell's Compass Point house and began planning the Wailers' next move.

Over the next few days, Rita and the Marley children along with the rest of the Wailers band arrived in Nassau. Everyone was glad to have made it to the relative safety of Nassau and a period of rest and healing began. Even as the band members were becoming rejuvenated, Don

Kinsey quit the band and returned to America. Kinsey had been shot in the attack on the house at 56 Hope Road and believed that the threat of violence persisted for Bob and those close to him.

Although the Wailers were not present to witness it, the Jamaican national election did take place on December 15, 1976, and PNP head Michael Manley remained the prime minister of the country (a position that he held until 1980). The 1976 election lead-up had been especially bloody. In addition to the violence perpetrated on the Wailers and their entourage, over two hundred Jamaicans died in the course of reelecting Manley. The island then descended into another period of simmering unrest in the wake of the election.

While the Wailers were isolated in Nassau, they were afforded a luxurious existence for the month of their stay. At the end of December, Bob's girlfriend Cindy Breakspeare came and visited the reggae superstar on Paradise Island (a smaller land mass that is connected to the northeast coast of Nassau). Together, the pair enjoyed each other's company and immersed themselves in their relationship. Soon, this relationship produced Bob's son Damian, his ninth child.

Although the lives of the Wailers were in peril in Jamaica, they felt safer elsewhere. When the band members were prepared to begin recording their next album, they went to London to see Blackwell and get to work. As Blackwell had provided their previous guitarists, he was the logical choice for a recommendation to replace Kinsey. He gave Bob the name of a black blues guitarist named Junior Marvin (who worked under the names Junior Kerr, Junior Hanson, and others. Marvin was Jamaican born, but raised in the United States. Further, he had the right musical credentials, having studied under American blues legend T. Bone Walker. When the Wailers arrived in London in 1977, Marvin was already at Island Studios recording with Steve Winwood. Marvin, Bob, and Blackwell met and Marvin was named the new Wailers' lead guitarist.

Through the early part of 1977, the Wailers remained in Blackwell's London studios working on their next record. The resulting tracks were paired down to 10 and titled *Exodus: Movement of Jah People*. Although in self-imposed exile from Jamaica, the group kept a careful watch on how musical style was changing on the island. New material was being released by bands such as the Itals, Israel Vibration, and Junior Murvin (of "Police and Thieves" fame). Even more significantly, the band Culture released its hit "Two Sevens Clash." The song became a huge hit in Jamaica and England with its discussion of Rastafarian millenarianism. Rastafarianism is one of several religions with millenarian beliefs that a major change will occur at the end of each 100-year cycle. Rastas believed that the current cycle was to end in 1977 and at that time the oppressive rule of the Babylon system would end.

EXODUS

During the *Exodus* session, Lee "Scratch" Perry turned up in London and Bob stopped the session to spend time catching up with his old friend and producer. Perry was able to update Bob on the evolution of the Jamaican music scene. He also asked Bob to record a song called "Punky Reggae Party." The song was written by Perry and was meant to cement the relationship between reggae and English punk music. An impromptu recording session ensued, and Bob's voice was backed by a collection of instrumentalists from the Third World band and the new English reggae group Aswad.

The relationship between reggae and punk existed from the mid-1970s, when the punk style began. Many early punk musicians found a particular kinship with those on the reggae scene, because both groups felt marginalized and oppressed by parliamentary-style governments that did not relate to the underclass. Musically, the two styles did not share many characteristics; however, several punk bands covered reggae standards and often adopted the reggae style. For example, Junior Murvin's hit single "Police and Thieves" was covered by the Clash and was a hit for both groups.

After Bob had completed his work with Perry, the *Exodus* sessions resumed. The band had already recorded 20 tracks and added another 10 in the second flurry of recording. The group then selected the 10 most expressive tracks for the album and on June 3, 1977, *Exodus* was released as the sixth Island Records/Wailers band product. The album included the tracks "Natural Mystic," "So Much Things to Say," "Guiltiness," "The Heathen," "Exodus," "Jamming," "Waiting in Vain," "Turn Your Lights Down Low," "Three Little Birds," and "One Love/People Get Ready." The makeup of the band for the release was the same as it had been for *Rastaman Vibration* with the substitution of Marvin for Kinsey on guitar. Also present on the album was the use of a new drumming style that was coming out of Jamaica. Popularized by Sly Dunbar, of the legendary duo Sly and Robbie, the drumming technique of evenly accenting all beats in a measure created songs called "rockers," and the title track of the album was of this sort.

The sentiments of the new record reflected Bob's post–assassination attempt mood. The opening song was called "Natural Mystic," which was one of Bob's nicknames and was used to herald his reappearance after the shooting. Next was a trio of songs whose lyrical content found Bob trying to come to a reconciliation with the events of December 1976. Each song built on its predecessor, and through the three Bob casts the finger of guilt around the island at those who sought to harm him. Although Bob was known for his kindness and his interest in universal love, these songs reveal how deeply had been wounded, when he warned his attackers that retribution would be swift and painful.

Bob also continued his previously noted interest in quoting Bible passages. The title track of the album took a serious tone that was enhanced through the rocker rhythm and the use of the Zap Pow horns. Here Bob decried the treatment of the Rastafarian faithful and calls for his brothers and sisters to repatriate. The concept of repatriation runs through Rastafarian belief, but it was not intended as a literal invitation to return to Africa. Instead, it was meant as a philosophical return to Africa, with its pride and majesty in one's head, regardless of one's location.

The rest of *Exodus* was a mixture of dance and love songs. "Jamming" was a lighthearted attempt to put the event of late 1976 behind the band. "Waiting in Vain," "Turn Your Lights Down Low," and "Three Little Birds" were all love songs expressing Bob's feelings for Breakspeare. The final track was the mixing of Bob's and Curtis Mayfield's (of the Impressions) songwriting. "One Love/People Get Ready" expressed universal love and unity with a hint of the American civil rights movement. The *Exodus* release was another huge success for the Wailers. The reaction to the album was so strong that all but three of the songs were released as singles, a feat that was not matched until Michael Jackson released *Thriller*.

EXODUS TOUR

As was now the custom, the Wailers next prepared to tour in support of *Exodus*. The band spent time preparing for what would be another long trip through Western Europe and North America. While the preparations for the tour were underway, Bob and Family Man ran afoul of the London police. The pair was stopped while driving through northwest London. They were searched and it was discovered that both men had large ganja spliffs in their possession. The police then searched the apartment where Bob had been staying (away from the place where the rest of the band was housed) and they uncovered approximately a pound of marijuana. Bob and Family Man were ordered to appear in court on charges of possessing (large quantities of) a controlled substance. Because neither man had been brought up on any previous charges, they escaped with a fine and a warning not to appear again in court for any reason.

While disappointed at his bad luck at the hands of the police, Bob's mood was brightened when he discovered that the Ethiopian royal family was living in exile in London at this time. Bob had occasion to meet Crown Prince Zere-Yacobe Asfa-Wossen, the pretender to his grandfather's throne (Haile Selassie I had been deposed on September 12, 1974; with his government in disarray, a group of low-ranking military officers had effectively overthrown the weakened leader and removed his family from the rulership of the country). The meeting had two outcomes. First, Wossen gave Bob a gold ring emblazoned with the golden Lion of Judah emblem, a ring that the reggae superstar wore for the rest of his life. Also, Bob's interest in Africa (specifically Ethiopia) was deepened significantly.

BOB'S FOOT INJURY

The Wailers launched the *Exodus* tour at Pavillon Baltard in Paris, France, on May 10, 1977. The tour was off to an immediate success, but tragedy struck when Bob's right big toe was badly injured in a soccer game. The game was a friendly match between members of the Wailers' entourage and a group of French journalists. The injury was significant and upon closer inspection, Bob realized that he should see a doctor. The doctor noted that Bob had lost most of his toenail and informed him that he needed to stay off of his feet to give the injury time to heal. Bob did not heed the doctor's warning as he was aware of the seriousness of canceling any prearranged tour obligations. Also, Rastafarians do not strictly adhere to modern medicine.

Despite the injury, Bob and the Wailers continued the European leg of the tour. The group played shows in Belgium, the Netherlands, and Denmark, four shows in Germany, two shows in Sweden, and wrapped up the European leg with five shows in England. The English dates included an appearance on the BBC show *Top of the Pops* and four shows at the Rainbow Theatre. With Marvin in the band, the Wailers live show was even more electrifying than it had been. At the end of the London shows, Bob was suffering from his failure to look after his injured foot. The toe injury had not been allowed to heal properly and Bob's onstage dancing had reopened the injury. With the European leg completed on June 4 and the American leg not scheduled to start until the Palladium show in New York in July, Bob went to his mother's house in Delaware to recuperate. With the support of the tour, *Exodus* had shot to number one on the English and German charts, and the pressure was on to make the record a hit in the United States.

Bob's foot seemed to be worsening instead of healing and he returned to London to see a foot specialist. The doctor gave Bob's foot a full examination, even collecting some skin cells for examination under a microscope. The doctor then informed Bob that the sample revealed mutated cancerous cells that could require the amputation of the affected toe. Bob asked the doctor to explore alternatives and soon learned that there was an alternative, but it had accompanying risks. Instead of amputating the toe, a small portion of it could be removed and the wound cleaned and redressed. This alternative still did not please Bob and he sought a second opinion in Miami.

Bob's toe was examined by Dr. William Bacon, the doctor who had operated on Taylor after the shooting at 56 Hope Road. Bacon seconded the London doctor's opinion, that a part of Bob's foot needed to be removed. On July 20, the American leg of the *Exodus* tour was postponed to allow Bob to undergo surgery. Although officially the tour was only postponed, all tickets were refunded and no dates were rescheduled. Bob's surgery was performed at Cedars of Lebanon Hospital in Miami, and all of the cancerous cells were removed. With all of the mutated cells removed, Bob recovered at a house that he purchased in Miami. The doctor's recommendation for Bob's recovery involved the singer returning to eating meat, for its protein. After two months of recovery and a new diet, Bob was well again and ready to return to the road.

Even without tour support, *Exodus* was a hit in the United States and the Wailers were revered on a par with America rock and roll's elite. During Bob's recovery, the Wailers had also joined him in Miami, and once the singer had regained his strength, the group entered Criteria Recording Studios, in Miami, to begin constructing a new record from the extra tracks recorded at the London sessions that had produced *Exodus*. The produce of these mixing and overdubbing sessions in Miami was the next Wailers album, *Kaya*. Also, Bob and Taylor were putting together another Wailers summer tour. This tour would span the world and attempt to make up for the canceled American shows.

While planning the Wailers' next activities and completing his recovery, Bob was also writing new songs. His thoughts were also occupied with concern for his island home. The unrest leading up to the 1976 election had continued after the election was held. The PNP's socialist leanings were only made worse through continued control of the island, and the growing lack of confidence in the Manley administration was tearing the country apart. The Rastafarians on the island, by belief a peaceful group, began the Jamaican peace movement at the beginning of 1978 with the hope that the ever-worsening violence could be stopped.

ONE LOVE JAMAICAN PEACE CONCERT

In a failed attempt to stem the violence on the island, Manley declared martial law, sent the Jamaican national army into the streets, and gave them the order that any known gunman should be immediately arrested. Two such political goons who were arrested and detained in the same cell were Bob Marley associates. Claudius ("Claudie" or "Jack") Massop and Bucky Marshall were both childhood friends of Bob in addition to being the ruthless enforcers for the two ruling parties (Massop for the JLP and Marshall for the PNP). Tired of being used as political pawns and gun fodder, Marshall and Massop began discussing the possibility of staging another concert for peace in Kingston. The two vowed to get their parties to commit to a ceasefire that would be accompanied by negotiations to end the bloodshed and a public concert to celebrate the island's changing circumstances. The plan behind the plan was that if the level of violence was reduced then the army would be removed from the streets and the whole situation could cool off.

While the idea was a good one, Bob was justifiably skeptical, as he was sure that members of one or both of the parties that Marshall and Massop represented were responsible for the attempt on his life. The two men promised the reggae superstar that they could guarantee his safety themselves. The circumstances were made more complicated by the fact that Bob had not yet returned to Jamaica. Marshall and Massop had a series of daunting obstacles to overcome. First, they had to get their warring, rival groups to agree to put aside their differences and then they needed to get Bob to return to the island to headline a concert.

To assist with Bob's return, Marshall and Massop spoke to the leader of the Twelve Tribes of Israel Rastafarian sect, Vernon "Gad the Prophet" Carrington. They believed that if the invitation came from the Twelve Tribes, it would be harder for Bob to refuse. Carrington was convinced and he sent members of his group to meet with Bob in London to discuss the peace accord and possible concert. By February, Massop was in London for his own meetings with Bob. Bob and Massop had grown up together and the two were friends. However, things became strained when Bob contended that Massop and the JLP could not ensure his health, even if they had in fact not been responsible for the assassination attempt. Massop told Bob that the attempt on his life had been for political reasons and that the JLP was to blame.

In addition to members of the Twelve Tribes and Massop, Bob also discussed the possibility of returning to Jamaica with PNP representative Tony Welsh, who had been sent to meet with Bob when the PNP learned that Massop was in London. This group met over the course of a week and discussed the details of a truce and the possibility of a concert. Bob finally conceded and agreed to play the concert, which effectively ended his exile from Jamaica. The concert was announced to the world press on February 23. The One Love Jamaican Peace Concert was scheduled for April 22, 1978. Bob Marley and the Wailers were booked to headline. Other artists that agreed to perform included original Wailer Peter Tosh, Jacob Miller and Inner Circle, the Mighty Diamonds, Trinity, Dennis Brown, Culture, Dillinger, Big Youth, and Ras Michael and the Sons of Negus.

As the Wailers were gearing up for another tour, they decided to use the Jamaican Peace Concert as the kickoff event for the tour. The band again went through a lineup change when Al Anderson returned on rhythm guitar and Earl "Wya" Lindo again joined the group on keyboards. In order to build additional hype for the concert and tour, the Wailers released their seventh Island Records release, *Kaya*. With the momentum building for the concert, tour, and new album, Bob returned to Jamaica after his 14-month exile.

Bob arrived back in Jamaica on February 26, 1978, with the expressed mission of bringing peace back to the island. The One Love Jamaican Peace Concert was scheduled for April 22 and the Twelve Tribes of Israel Rastafarian brotherhood was the sponsor of record. The concert was not intended for any political posturing; instead it was meant to undo years of damage caused by the infighting that had created the current state of meltdown. The fact that the warring JLP and PNP factions had agreed to a tenuous ceasefire indicated that even the political goon squads were concerned about the level of bloodshed. The tension in Kingston was intense, illustrated by the constant presence of the police, wearing bulletproof vests and carrying shotguns, in the yard of the house at 56 Hope Road.

The concert date dawned and all of Jamaica's most significant bands were slated to perform. The tense mood of the period leading up to the concert was continued at the show with hundreds of policemen in attendance. As band after band took the stage in front of the audience of more than 32,000 people, the anticipation grew. Peter Tosh's set was incendiary as he criticized the government, calling it the "shitstem," instead of the system. Tosh also flaunted his onstage freedom when he lit up a large spliff from the stage, even as police and government officials looked on helplessly. He continued his rebellion, yelling at the crowd that he did not want peace, but instead wanted equality. He blazed through seven songs and then Ras Michael and the Sons of Negus played a five-song set. The concert climaxed when the Wailers took the stage as the final act.

Bob walked on stage dressed in a brown burlap pullover shirt with a map of Africa on the back, decorated in many colors. At his entrance the crowd erupted in loud applause, having been left doubting that he would ever return to the island. Bob and the Wailers gave a legendary 50-minute performance with a nine-song set list. That night they played the songs "Lion of Judah" (which they rarely played live), "Natural Mystic," "Trench Town Rock," "Natty Dread," "Positive Vibration," "War," "Jamming," "One Love/People Get Ready," and "Jah Live."

During the performance of the song "Jamming," Bob began an extended skat vocal (skat singing is vocal improvisation in which the words are made up on the spot or nonsense syllables are used such as "doo" and "wop"). Bob sang:

> To make everything come true, we've got to be together, yeah, yeah. And to the spirit of the most high, His Imperial Majesty Emperor Haile Selassie I, run lightning, leading the people of the slaves to shake hands....I'm trying to say, could we have, could we have, up here onstage here the presence of Mr. Michael Manley and Mr. Edward Seaga. I just want to shake hands and show the people that we're gonna unite....we're gonna unite....we've got to unite.

With this invitation, opposition leaders Seaga and Manley exited the front row of the audience, where they had been seated, and ascended the stairs to the stage. Bob took one hand of each man and joined them over his head in a show of unity. While both men were visibly uncomfortable with the situation, Bob reveled in the physical union of the two rival powers. In addition to the pleasure Bob got from the PNP and JLP peace meeting, he was overjoyed when his children joined him on stage during the final song of the Wailers' set.

KAYA

After the One Love Peace Concert, the Wailers geared up for an international tour in support of the *Kaya* record. The album represented a different side of Bob that he had not previously revealed in such a systematic manner. Although the tracks on the album were recorded in London, during the same sessions that yielded *Exodus*, the *Kaya* material was not militant and the album was instead filled with mellow dance music. The name of the album is Rastafarian slang for marijuana and the album content paid homage to the Rastafarian wisdom weed. In fact, the first song on the album began with the words "'cuse [excuse] me while I light my spliff."

The album jacket showed a grainy picture of a smiling Bob, while the back of the jacket displayed a colorful picture of a large spliff. Contained on the album were the songs "Easy Skanking," "Kaya," "Is This Love," "Sun Is Shining," "Satisfy My Soul," "She's Gone," "Misty Morning," "Crisis," "Running Away," and "Time Will Tell." The persons performing on the album were the same as had been present on *Exodus*. In the wake of the album's release, Bob went to New York to meet with the press and music critics.

KAYA TOUR

The Wailers then began their world tour in support of the record. The tour had three parts, two North American legs with one European leg that separated them. Many houses were sold out, and several performances were recorded for posterity using Blackwell's own Island Mobile Studio. The tour was scheduled to begin in Miami, Florida, on May 5, 1978. However, the first six dates were canceled. Some reports indicate that this cancellation was due to unspecified problems with Junior Marvin's health; others speculated that the Wailer guitarist was struggling with cocaine addiction. The tour then began in earnest in Ann Arbor, Michigan. Shows followed throughout the Midwest, followed by a swing out to the East Coast and then north into Canada for a pair of shows. The group then returned to the United States for another series of American dates before departing for the European leg of the tour.

The European leg began in England with a show at the New Bingley Hall in Staffordshire. Next, the tour crossed into France for three dates before it headed to Ibiza, Spain, Sweden for two shows, Denmark, Norway, and the Netherlands for two shows. The European leg ended with a stop in Belgium and a return to England for another appearance on *Top of the Pops*.

The second North American leg of the tour began in Vancouver, British Columbia, and then came south into Washington, Oregon, followed by six shows in California. The highlight of the California shows was on July 21, at the Starlight Amphitheater in Burbank, when Tosh jumped on stage during the encore for an unexpected duet. The band then crossed the southern part of the United States, performing the six shows that had been canceled at the beginning of the tour. The popularity of *Kaya* was assured through the lengthy tour. The album yielded two hit singles,

"Is This Love" and "Satisfy My Soul." These songs were also released as videos to further enhance their promotion.

Still in Miami at the end of the tour, Bob recorded a song by Jamaican producer King Sporty. The song was called "Buffalo Soldier," and its lyrics connected the Rastafarian struggles to those of the black soldiers in the U.S. cavalry during the Indian Wars. Noel G. Williams, known as King Sporty, owned his own Tashamba and Konduko record labels and was a Jamaican DJ and reggae musician.

BABYLON BY BUS

An offshoot of the recording of several of the Wailers shows from the *Kaya* tour was the release of another live album. Blackwell headed into the studio with the raw tapes of Wailers shows from Paris, Copenhagen, London, and Amsterdam. He emerged with the master tapes for the live album *Babylon by Bus*. Released in 1978, the album included 13 exemplary live performances including the songs "Positive Vibrations," "Punky Reggae Party," "Exodus," "Stir It Up," "Rat Race," "Concrete Jungle," "Kinky Reggae," "Lively Up Yourself," "Rebel Music," "War/No More Trouble," "Is This Love," "The Heathen," and "Jamming."

The album began with an introduction by Bob during which he continued to assert his faith in Haile Selassie I. He welcomed the crowd in the name of Ras Tafari. He went on to repeat that Selassie was "ever living" and "ever sure." Bob further linked himself with Selassie through repeated use of the "I and I" word choice of Rastafarians. He then engaged in a brief call and response with the audience that led into the first track. The album captured the Wailers at a new height of live performance, and the power of Bob's singing and his vocal presence illustrated how far the singer had come since the *Live!* album was released three years earlier.

A strange circumstance unfolded with the release of the *Babylon by Bus* album: the Wailers toured in support of a live album without releasing any new studio material. The group was capable of doing this because its international reputation had grown to such a high level and there were still parts of the world in which it had not performed. In pursuit of newer and larger audiences, the Wailers launched the *Babylon by Bus* tour, with the idea that they would play parts of the world that had not been previously exposed to live reggae music.

Chapter 4

REGGAE INTERNATIONAL

The tour was booked and the Wailers prepared to embark on their first tour of the Far East and the Pacific Rim. The first two dates of the tour were scheduled for Abidjan in the Ivory Coast. Both of these dates were canceled for unknown reasons. However, Bob continued to pursue Wailers appearances in Africa, even with this initial disappointment. The tour then started on April 5, 1979, with a series of eight shows in Japan. From Japan, the Wailers traveled to Auckland, New Zealand, for an appearance. Bob was greeted by a collection of aboriginal Maoris who treated him like a king and related their struggles with an oppressive white government to those of the Jamaica underclass. The New Zealand show was followed by an eight-show stand in Australia. Next, the group flew to Hawaii for two shows before returning to Jamaica.

Bob now planned his next move. He had several albums worth of material in his head that he had composed while on the road. Also, he was obsessed with booking a Wailers concert in Ethiopia. Having spent long hours thinking about and discussing the black fatherland, Bob believed that the Wailers' next big tour must include an African appearance. He had been hampered in his efforts by the ongoing war between Ethiopia and the territory directly to the north called Eritrea. The 30-year war for Eritrean independence lasted from 1961 to 1991 and the war meant that Bob could not get a visa to travel to Ethiopia.

BOB IN AFRICA

Coincidentally, as Bob was trying to enter Ethiopia, Alan "Skill" Cole had turned up in the Ethiopian capital, Addis Ababa. Cole had apparently fled to Africa in the wake of the assassination attempt in Kingston. He had used his soccer-playing credentials to get a coaching job with the Ethiopian Airlines soccer team. Bob was finally awarded a visa in late 1978 and together he and Cole planned a trip to Ethiopia.

Bob left Jamaica and flew to London, then Nairobi, and then on to Ethiopia. Once there, he visited several places of significance to him, most importantly sites connected with Haile Selassie I. Bob also spent time on a religious communal farm called Shashamani, attended a rally in support of the liberation movement in Rhodesia, and spent time soaking up the local nightlife. Based on these experiences, Bob began to work on the song "Zimbabwe," the African name being used for Rhodesia during the struggle for internationally recognized independence from long-standing white minority rule.

Bob returned from Africa refreshed and ready to get back to work. He had albums worth of material in his head ready for recording, and his renewed faith in black unity gave a serious edge to his new music. While he had been away, his lawyer Diane Jobson ran the ever-growing Tuff Gong empire. This was no small task as she was charged with the day-to-day management of the only multimillion-dollar music company in the third world.

The Wailers returned to the studio and their first product was the single "Ambush in the Night." The song was released on the Tuff Gong imprint in early 1979 and reflected Bob's steadfast resolve. Here, Bob again addressed his would-be assassins, holding them in check because he was protected by Selassie's divinity.

While busy in the studio and with Tuff Gong business, Bob was still aware that the tenuous post–One Love Freedom Concert peace had been broken. His old friend Claudie Massop was returning from a February soccer match when he was stopped at a police roadblock. Reports indicate that Massop was unarmed and approached officers on the scene with his hands in the air. The officers opened fire and Massop was reportedly shot 44 times. With acts such as this, the uneasy peace that had been present on the island since the One Love Peace Concert was shattered. The reasons for Massop's execution were never substantiated, but rumors swirled that he had stolen the money from the Peace concert.

Another of Bob's long-time island friends, Lee "Scratch" Perry, suffered a nervous breakdown and was briefly institutionalized at Kingston's Belleview Hospital. However, amid the chaos of 1979, Bob worked diligently to finish recording his next album. Another Wailers tour had already been planned and Bob wanted to finish recording the new material before the tour began. During this period, even amid the turmoil, Bob found some peace in his life. He worked diligently on his new record, but also took long hours to play soccer and spend time with his children. Also, with Yvette Morris, he fathered his 11th child, a daughter named Makeba (the Queen of Sheba) Jahnesta.

SURVIVAL

Part of the 1979 recording process was Bob's introduction to a new Blackwell-assigned producer, Alex Sadkin. Sadkin was trained as an audio mastering engineer and became a well-known music producer through his work at Criteria Studios in Miami and at Blackwell's Compass Point Studios in Nassau, Bahamas. Although he had a short life (he died in 1987 in an auto accident at age 35), he recorded material for the Talking Heads, Joe Cocker, James Brown, Marianne Faithfull, and others. His work with Bob resulted in the *Survival* album. Released in the summer of 1979, the working title of the album had been *Black Survival*, inspired by Bob's trip to Africa.

The album itself contained songs on topics such as rebellion, religion, and escape from oppression. Containing 10 songs in all, the album collected some of Bob's most personal commentary on his life and the world surrounding him. The tracks contained on the album were "So Much Trouble in the World," "Zimbabwe," "Top Rankin'," "Babylon System," "Survival," "Africa Unite," "One Drop," "Ride Natty Ride," "Ambush in the Night," and "Wake Up and Live." On this record, Bob was the leader of the oppressed black man in the Western world. He sang of removing the oppressors' chains and the dawning of a new era in which black freedom and global harmony for the black race existed. He was the Rastafarian warrior on a mission to reunite and bring peace to the African diaspora.

REGGAE SUNSPLASH

With the album complete, the Wailers again geared up for an extended summer tour. They kicked the tour off with a headlining appearance in the Reggae Sunsplash II concert held at Jarrett Park in Montego Bay in early July 1979. The Reggae Sunsplash concert series had been in part Bob's idea and began in 1978. The Wailers would certainly have participated in the inaugural performance, but it took place while the group was off the island during the *Kaya* tour.

During the second incarnation of the concert, the Wailers were the natural headliners. The show was history-making in quality, although rain made the venue a mud puddle and hampered the group's performance.

The concert was a huge success with an international audience in attendance. Because of this success and the international appeal, the Reggae Sunsplash concert series continues currently. Each year the best of Jamaican reggae talent is recruited for a show on the island. This show then serves as the beginning of an extensive tour promoting Jamaican music around the world.

Historically, the Reggae Sunsplash concerts have been enormously successful and have exposed the world to Jamaican music start such as Third World, Culture, Steel Pulse, Toots and the Maytals, Freddie McGregor, Morgan Heritage, Buju Banton, Beenie Man, Elephant Man, and others. The series of concerts stopped in 1999 when the driving force behind them, Tony Johnson, died. However, the Reggae Sunsplash show reemerged with a three-day festival held on August 3–6, 2006. The plans are again to make the concert an annual event, and planning for future festivals is already underway.

SURVIVAL TOUR

With this auspicious start, the Bob Marley and the Wailers' 25-member member *Survival* touring group left Jamaica for an extended American tour. From Jamaica, the Wailers traveled to Boston, Massachusetts, to perform in the Amandla Festival at Harvard University. Amandla is a shorted form of the phrase meaning "power to the people" in the Shona language of Zimbabwe. This concert, called the Festival of Unity, was organized by Chester England to benefit the Amandla group, whose mission was to support African liberation and freedom fighters. The show included luminaries from around the world, such as American soul singer Patti Labelle, and 25,000 people attended. The Amandla show started with the song "Exodus" and ended with "Zimbabwe" and "Wake Up and Live." Throughout, Bob was the voice of African freedom. During "Wake Up and Live," Bob began to scat a speech to the audience that included discussion of brotherhood, unity, and concern over conditions in Africa. The concert earned almost a quarter of a million dollars for the cause of African liberation.

The tour then rolled on with a series of dates in the United States that began with an appearance at Madison Square Garden with the Commodores and the rap legend Kurtis Blow. The band then had a four-day stand at New York's Apollo Theater. Bob had purposely established this set of shows in the historically black and lower-class section of New York. By attracting the attention of the residents of Harlem, Bob believed that his music could truly cross over to a black American audience. Soon, he learned that these shows had had a deep impact and he was being talked about extensively in black American listening circles.

During this period, the *Survival* album was officially released. In contrast to the commercial fare that had been *Kaya*, *Survival* was pure militant reggae and illustrated Bob at his highest potency. In addition to Bob's long-standing discussions of freedom for blacks in Jamaica, the new album now included discussions of freedom for all black people regardless of location. This Pan-African theme was woven into the fabric of Bob's music and life for the rest of his time on earth. Bob also continued to deliver his message through his long-evolving preference for the quotation of Bible passages.

The *Survival* album itself was a testament to Bob's convictions. The front cover of the album contained small-scale examples of the flags of all of the African nations circa 1979. At the top of the front cover was a banner displaying the layout for stowage of African slaves as they were transported in ships from Africa to the Americas. Superimposed over this was the album's title. The back cover continued the slave ship banner and included the titles of the songs contained on the album.

The lineup for the album included the Wailers regulars from the previous recording. However, there was one significant addition: Carlton "Santa" Davis played drums on several key tracks. Davis had played in several of the island's most famous bands in the pre-Marley era, such as Soul Syndicate. He is also credited with appearances with almost all important Jamaican popular groups since the 1970s, including Jimmy Cliff, Black Uhuru, Burning Spear, Big Youth, Peter Tosh, Ini Kamoze, Big Mountain, and many others. For the *Survival* sessions, Santa sat in with the Wailers on the song "Africa Unite." Santa is certainly a Jamaican reggae icon in his own right, but his association with the Wailers on the *Survival* and *Uprising* releases illustrated that he is among the most sought after musicians on the island.

SURVIVAL TOUR CONTINUED

The *Survival* tour continued when the group headed north into Canada before returning to the United States for several East Coast appearances. Although unwilling to let it stop him, Bob had been fighting a cold since starting the *Survival* tour. Incredibly, the cold would stay with him throughout the tour. In Philadelphia, on November 7, Stevie Wonder joined the Wailers on stage to sing "Get Up, Stand Up" and "Exodus." The Wailers then pressed on into the Midwest on their way to the West Coast. The Midwest dates included stops in Michigan, Wisconsin, Illinois, and Minnesota.

The Wailers again crossed the border for a show in Alberta, Canada, before beginning their trip south along the western coast of the United States. As had been the case on previous tours, the Wailers were most enthusiastically received in California. They played eight California concerts as the tour continued through the fall. While in California, Bob's health improved. However, he seemed constantly tired and increasingly passed off his duties, such as giving interviews, to other members of the band. The group then crossed the southern part of the country with only a few stops. The *Survival* tour drew to a close as the year ended. The band played for the first time in Trinidad and Tobago and concluded the tour in Nassau with an appearance at the Queen Elizabeth Sports Center.

In addition to the strong start to the tour, with the headlining appearance on the Reggae Sunsplash II concert and the Amandla success, the *Survival* tour had several other highlights. The performance in Santa Barbara, California, on November 25, was recorded and eventually released as on VHS (later remastered to DVD). Also, the concert in Oakland, California, on November 30, featured a guest appearance by Rolling Stones guitarist Ron Wood. The final concert of the tour, at the Queen Elizabeth Sports Center in Nassau, was presented as a benefit concert for the children in the Bahamas as part of the International Year of the Child. That night, Bob donated the royalties form the song "Children Playing in the Streets" to the cause. Bob had written the song for four of his own children—Ziggy, Stephen, Sharon, and Cedella—who went on to form their own musical group called the Melody Makers, and the group also recorded the song.

UPRISING

Philosophically, the *Survivor* album was a part of a larger puzzle that Bob was trying to construct. With the sounds and messages of the album, Bob laid the groundwork for his "call to action" for all black people. This message came in three installments as conceived by the songwriter. The second part of the trilogy was the next album, *Uprising*. The third, although released posthumously, was the album *Confrontation*. Bob was careful about how he delivered his thoughts on black action. The first step was to survive four hundred years of persecution at the hands of white oppressors; next, the disenfranchised black population must band together and shake loose their shackles (either literally or figuratively); and third, they should make the move to a location where they could be free to live in peace (Africa). Even during the *Survival* tour, Bob was writing the words for new songs that followed his philosophical trajectory.

Bob's vision became a reality, at least in part. Due to the message in the song "Zimbabwe," African freedom fighters adopted the tune as a rallying point. Zimbabwe's Patriotic Front used the song to buoy their spirits during the long fight for freedom and considered Bob a kindred spirit from whom they drew strength. The song gave word to the reasons why many of the soldiers were fighting the war at all and united them in a solidarity that would eventually lead to victory. This type of prophecy through song went far to enhance Bob's reputation both during his life and in death. Bob Marley was soon known as the international voice of freedom and he was quickly adopted by oppressed people everywhere (regardless of color) as a figure to rally around.

As the *Survivor* tour and 1979 came to a close, Bob and the Wailers worked to set up the band's schedule for the new year. They had already planned a band trip to Africa, time in London, and recording sessions for the next album. As expected, the release of *Uprising* would also spawn a massive tour. This had several purposes. First, it was meant to expose the Wailers' music to an even wider audience. Second, it served the purpose of keeping Bob out of Jamaica for the general election of 1980. And third, it was to take the Wailers to Africa for the first time. The coordination of such a variety of activities was a major step. For these purposes, Bob renamed his company Tuff Gong International, as an indication of their ever-broadening worldview.

UPRISING TOUR

Because the Wailers toured in advance of the U.S. release of the *Uprising* album, officially June 10, 1980, the band was already playing the new songs before the audience had heard them on the recording. The *Uprising* tour entourage left Kingston on January 1, 1980, and traveled first to London and then on to Libreville, Gabon, in western Africa. The country of Gabon is on the west coast of the African continent. It is bordered by Equatorial Guinea, Cameroon, the Republic of Congo, and the Gulf of Guinea. Officially called the Gabonese Republic, the country achieved independence from France only in 1960. Since then, its president has been El Hadj Omar Bongo Ondimba (who currently has the distinction of being a very long serving head of state). The country has a limited population and abundant natural resources that make it among the most prosperous in the region.

The Wailers had been booked to play for the president's birthday and the band's excitement was palpable. With this trip, Bob was realizing one of his longest-sought goals. The show was also meant to expose the Wailers' music to a previously uninitiated group of people. The band was scheduled to play two shows. Bob was immensely excited about performing in Africa; he had initially said that he would pay for the touring expenses himself as long as the Bongo family paid for the actual Wailers appearance. He then left it to his manager Don Taylor to make all of the appropriate arrangements with the oil-rich Bongo family.

RETURN TO AFRICA

The Wailers' touring unit, and their opener Betty Wright, arrived in Africa and were dismayed to learn that they were not to play for the general public at all. Instead, they had been slated to perform in a small tennis area for only 2,000 of the Gabonese elite. Although Bob was unhappy with the arrangement, he was pleased when, during the group's two-week stay; young Gabonese citizens approached him to discuss Rastafarianism. After the Wailers had played the contracted two shows, the band prepared to leave. This meant that it was time to be paid for the engagements. A dispute arose concerning the agreed-upon fee. Bob had established with Taylor that the Wailers would be paid a total of $40,000 for the two appearances. Taylor was apparently demanding a fee of $60,000, with the suspected aim of pocketing the other $20,000 for himself.

A Bongo family representative heard that he was being blamed for the misunderstanding and immediately went to Bob to straighten things out. Bob reasoned with the man and learned of Taylor's deceit. Not only had Taylor marred an otherwise good African experience for the Wailers, but he had cast doubt on Bob's character in the eyes of the Gabonese elite. Bob straightened everything out with the Bongo family and their representative, and then he and Taylor had a huge fight.

During their three-hour argument, Taylor reportedly blamed the whole thing on the Bongo family representative. Nevertheless, Bob was inconsolable. The exact facts of the blowup are not clear, but the result of Bob and Taylor's fight was that Taylor finally admitted to mishandling Bob's money. He had established a long-running practice of receiving as much as $15,000 per show as an advance and passing along only $5,000 to Bob and the band. Taylor also admitted to stealing from the Wailers in another manner. Bob would give Taylor money, sometimes as much as $50,000 at once, for Taylor to transfer to Family Man back in Jamaica. Taylor then exchanged this money on the black market for as much as three times its face value. He then kept the ill-gotten gains and gave Family Man only the original amount. The Wailers' manager was apparently not ready to give this information and while reports conflict, it is possible that Bob had to beat a confession out of him. Once Bob knew the truth and the nature of the betrayal, he demanded that Taylor return the money. Of course, the crooked band manager could not produce his illegal gains, saying that he had lost all the money gambling. This left Bob no choice: again burned by the music business, Bob fired Don Taylor and he and his band left Gabon.

The Taylor incident was just the worst of many examples of people in the music industry preying on Bob. He had had trouble getting properly paid for his music since he first began recording. This led to a general detestation for members of the music business and worsened Bob's disdain for those in power. Over the course of his career, Bob had only one successful relationship with a music industry insider. This successful union was with Christopher Blackwell, the Island Records label boss. Although Bob and Blackwell's relationship sometimes fell on hard times, it was with Blackwell's help that Bob reached international fame.

From Africa, the Wailers returned to Jamaica and set about the job of recording new material. Bob had enough new material in his head that these sessions produced sufficient tracks for two full-length albums. The first record that was produced from these recordings was titled *Uprising*. It was released in June 1980 and represented Bob in one of his more militant phases. His lyrical content was peppered with biblical quotes and his messages spoke strongly of unity and redemption. His experience in Africa was evident in the new material, and the band's sound was heavier to reflect Bob's mood.

The cover of the *Uprising* album depicted a triumphant dreadlocked black man with his hands raised in the traditional "V" for victory stance. His locks were so long that they framed the album title, which appeared at his waist. Behind him was an image of the sun raising over the top of a green mountain (possibly representing the Blue Mountains of Jamaica). The album tracks have been critically acclaimed as some of Marley's best work. The songs on the album are "Coming in from the Cold," "Real Situation," "Bad Card," "We and Dem," "Work," "Zion Train," "Pimper's Paradise," "Could You Be Loved," "Forever Loving Jah," and "Redemption Song."

The collection was filled with solid gold hits. In the years since its release, *Uprising* has become essential listening for all reggae and Bob Marley fans. Performing on the album were Bob, the Barrett brothers as the rhythm section, the I-Threes, Junior Marvin, Tyrone Downie, Alvin "Seeco" Patterson, and Earl "Wya" Lindo. The songs were all recorded and mixed at Tuff Gong Studios in Kingston, Jamaica. The 10-song testament to Bob's philosophy has only grown more intense with age.

The songs on the album reference Bob's life and point an accusatory finger in the direction of those who mistreated or wronged him. Bob's Rastafarianism was evident on almost all of the tracks. Biblical quotations and paraphrases were also present in most songs. Other themes present were unity, love, and cooperation. Due to the rough quality of Bob's voice on this album, several biographers have speculated that Bob knew that his health was not good and that he would not live much longer.

The album contained several standout tracks with autobiographical lyrics. "Bad Card" was Bob's chronicle of his experiences with Don Taylor. Taylor was literally the "bad card" that Bob drew and with which he "made wrong moves" in his business dealings. "Work" was another of Bob's calls to action for all oppressed people. The song was structured as a reverse counting song in which Bob counted down from five. The countdown represented the period until the ultimate goal of freedom was reached. The song ended with Bob declaring that Jah's people can make it work.

Bob's use of biblical quotations and paraphrases in his lyrics reached a new height on *Uprising*. Here Bob repeatedly evoked biblical sentiment, story, and prophecy through repeated use of the psalms. An example of this was found in the most popular song from the *Uprising* album, "Redemption Song." In this song, Marley created a series of images. First he placed himself in a colonial-era slave ship, then he quickly shifted to biblical language from Psalm 88, describing being cast into a bottomless pit. Bob also made use of text from Matthew 24:34 in the song, when he referred to killing prophets, and he again allied himself with Joseph through the use of text from Genesis 49:24. In the song, Bob was able to overcome these difficult scenarios through the help of almighty Jah. Another interesting feature of the song was that it was Bob's only track recorded without a backing band. Here Bob was at his most personal, singing with only an acoustic guitar for support. Although he did not know it at the time, "Redemption Song" was the last song that Bob would release during his life.

After the sessions that produced *Uprising* were completed, Bob briefly visited Miami. He was tired and wanted to rest, plus he needed to straighten out his management situation, as he was gearing up for another extended Wailers tour. At the same time, he was also acutely aware that his most recent album fulfilled his record contract with Island. So, in addition to needing a new manager, he was also soon to be without a record deal. In Miami, Bob met with Danny Sims, who made it clear that Bob's recording interests would be better served by switching labels and moving to Polygram Records. Bob opted to stick with Blackwell's Island Records label. Interestingly, Polygram eventually purchased Island

Records in a 1989 merger. In 1998, Seagram bought Polygram and absorbed it into the Universal Music Group.

BOB TURNS 35

In the face of all of this tumult, Bob decided to blow off a little steam and he threw himself a massive 35th birthday party. The part was held on February 6, 1980, at the house at 56 Hope Road. For the bash, Bob surrounded himself with his friends and family and paid special attention to all of the children gathered in the Hope Road yard. Frequently in Bob's life, he was captured in photographs interacting with children. It was clear from these images that Bob's often gruff exterior melted away when he was in the company of children.

While in Jamaica celebrating his birthday, Bob again noticed a change in the music of his island home. The reggae style behind which he was the driving force was being influenced by a new style called "rub-a-dub." The most popular example of this style in 1980 was the duo Papa Michigan and General Smiley. Michigan and Smiley were born Anthony Fairclough and Erroll Bennett and emerged on the Jamaican popular music scene as two of the earliest dual DJ outfits. They recorded with Bob's old producer Clement "Coxsone" Dodd and had instant success. Their notable songs from this time were "Rub a Dub Style" and "Nice Up the Dance." The pair realized Bob's star power and switched over to his Tuff Gong Records imprint.

The rub-a-dub style was very popular in the early 1980s and was characterized by a fast tempo, heavy use of the bass drum on beats two and four, and DJ toasting. Toasting was the Jamaican predecessor to rapping in New York and was achieved when DJs delivered improvised lyrics over a prerecorded beat. The beats were taken from "dub plates," which were the B-sides of Jamaican singles released with the words removed. The emergence of rub-a-dub, the shift of Michigan and Smiley to Tuff Gong, and the Jamaican practice of toasting were just of few of the exciting changes in the Jamaican music industry in the early 1980s.

At the same time, Jamaica was again descending into politically motivated violence. Bob was aware of this dangerous situation and kept to himself while on the island. His entourage and family were always around him, but he was careful to avoid a repeat of the 1976 attempt on his life. Security was maintained around the reggae superstar through the help of the Twelve Tribes of Israel Rastafarian brotherhood. During the run-up to the elections of 1980, PNP and JLP clashes resulted in 750 deaths, and several polling stations never opened on the election day due to the fear

of violence. Realizing that the Jamaican situation was getting out of control, Bob retreated to Miami to plan his next move.

While in Miami, Bob learned that Bucky Marshall had been shot and
killed at a block party in Brooklyn, New York, which made Bob uneasy
even in the United States. This difficult situation was quickly tempered
by joy when Bob and the band were invited to perform as part of the independence day celebrations for the newly established African country of
Zimbabwe.

Bob was aware that his song "Zimbabwe" had become quite popular in
Africa and that it was a rallying cry for the disenfranchised on the African
continent. However, he was awed by the invitation to return to Africa for
the purposes of helping to officially declare the existence of a new African nation. The leaders of the country formerly known as Rhodesia had
realized that the political situation was too unstable to continue. In the
mid-1960s, Ian Smith had set up a white minority party and declared unofficial independence from the British government. Smith was apposed by
Robert Mugabe and his Zimbabwe African National Union (ZANU) and
Joshua Nkomo's Zimbabwe African People's Union (ZAPU). In 1980,
this conflict came to a head and a general election was held. Mugabe and
ZANU won a landslide victory, England gave up any colonial ties to the
country, and Rhodesia was officially renamed Zimbabwe.

Bob Marley and the Wailers were the proud headliners of the Independence Day celebrations that marked the official inauguration of Zimbabwe as a free African nation. Mugabe's general secretary, Edgar Tekere,
contacted Bob to invite him to be one of the officiating dignitaries at the
independence celebrations, as his music had played such a key role in
emboldening the spirits of the Zimbabwean freedom fighters. After the
formal invitation to attend the celebration had been delivered, Bob was
visited by two African businessmen who invited him and the Wailers to
perform as part of the event. Bob was so honored by this that he made a
commitment to having the Wailers perform and he promised to pay the
band's travel expenses himself. He likely still had the Don Taylor/Gabon
fiasco in his head when he made these arrangements.

Although Bob and the band were ecstatic about their invitation to
Zimbabwe, they were in serious difficulty. The invitation had arrived
with very short notice and the lack of a band manager had not yet been
resolved. Regardless, Bob and the group pressed on, and three days later
they landed at Salisbury Airport. The country's capital city was called
Salisbury, but was being renamed Harare. The Wailers were met at the
airport by Joshua Nkomo, who had been the leader of the ZAPU movement and had been made Mugabe's minister of home affairs. Bob was

amazed that he was also greeted by Mugabe himself and Britain's Prince Charles. Mugabe was on hand to officially welcome Bob and the band and Prince Charles was the British representative who would lower his country's flag for the last time during the independence ceremony.

ZIMBABWE FREEDOM CONCERT

Shortly after the Wailers were welcomed in Salisbury/Harare, a Boeing 707 filled with equipment arrived. Twenty-one tons of Wailers' gear, staging, lights, and a 25,000-watt amplification system with 20 foot tall speaker boxes were unloaded and set up by a 12-man road crew. Bob Marley and the Wailers were preparing to give one of their most memorable performances in their ancestral homeland. The concert appearance was marked by the members of the band as the highest musical honor of their careers.

The concert was set for April 18, 1980, and during the independence day celebrations Rhodesia officially became Zimbabwe. The Wailers again assumed that they would be performing for the African masses and were disappointed to learn that they were slotted to perform immediately after the independence ceremony for an audience of dignitaries, including Mugabe, Prince Charles, and India's Indira Gandhi. Bob Marley and the Wailers took the stage at 8:30 in the evening, immediately after Zimbabwe's new national flag was raised for the first time.

When the Wailers played their first notes in the Rufaro Stadium on the edge of the capital city, pandemonium broke loose. A massive crowd had assembled outside the gates of the venue and when they heard the band begin to play they rushed the gates. Excited and expectant, the crowd was too big to control, and the national security force launched tear gas directly into the crush of gate crashers. Bob and the band were removed from the stage while order was restored. Once the crowd had been controlled, the Wailers retook the stage. They were told that they had only two more minutes in their allotted time and immediately cut into a scorching performance of "War." With their time elapsed, the band then broke into "No More Trouble," followed by the show stopper "Zimbabwe." The Wailers' set ended with all in attendance singing along to the chorus of the de facto national anthem of the newborn country.

After their set, the Wailers agreed to play another concert the next day. Over 100,000 people saw the Wailers perform the day after Zimbabwe achieved its independence. The band staged a 90-minute set of Wailers classics. However, Bob, who had been noticeably shaken the previous day by the tear gas incident, did not seem his usual self during the performance.

After the concerts in Zimbabwe, the Wailers left Africa, and on the plane several members of the entourage noticed that Bob did not appear healthy. His complexion was ashen and he did not look well.

After the performance in Zimbabwe in April, the Wailers launched the tour in support of their *Uprising* album in May. The tour was slated to be the biggest Wailers' undertaking yet. They were set to play in a variety of locations that they had not previously visited, such as Switzerland, Ireland, Scotland, and Italy. The tour schedule was rigorous, with six shows per week and each show set for a different city. Over the course of the tour the band played for over a million people, a feat that few have repeated since.

The tour began at the Hallenstadion in Zurich, Switzerland. It was a first for the band, which was well received by a new crowd. Next the group traveled to Germany for a show at the Horse Riding Stadium in Munich. The group was the opening act for Fleetwood Mac as part of the Munich Festival on June 1. The tour then alternated pairs of shows between Germany and France for two weeks. The Dortmund, Germany, show on June 12 was staged at the Westfalen Stadium and was broadcast on German TV and recorded on video for posterity. While touring, Bob was again writing new music. One example was the song "Slogans," which was not released until November 8, 2005, on the album *Africa Unite: The Singles Collection*. The song was a testament to the political lies and posturing that continually led Jamaica into violent upheaval.

After leaving Germany for the third time during the tour, the Wailers performed shows in Norway, Sweden, Denmark, Belgium, and Holland. They reentered France for a pair of concerts and then moved on to Italy. Two shows in Italy exposed the band to another new audience before the Wailers moved on to Spain, France again, Ireland, England, and Scotland. The concert in Milan, Italy, on June 27 was performed for an audience in excess of 120,000 people who had crammed into the sold-out San Siro Stadium. Incredibly, this show is still regarded as the most highly attended music event staged in Italy. After a month of European dates, the Wailers embarked for the American leg of the tour.

Leaving Europe, Bob returned to Miami for two months between the two parts of the tour. Without management, Bob's financial affairs were in ruin and things were only getting worse. Further, in the wake of the spilt with Taylor, Bob had sued his ex-manager for a million dollars and Taylor had countersued. All of this was made worse when Bob learned that he could not return to Jamaica to see his children because the island had again been plunged into violence leading up to the election. In Miami, Bob spoke to Danny Sims, who warned him sternly of the negative consequences of returning to Jamaica. Sims believed that Bob's reappearance on the island at this time would be viewed as an endorsement of the Manley PNP government and his life would again be in jeopardy. Although this news was grave, Sims did tell Bob that he had been brokering a deal for the Wailers to move to Polygram Records, a deal that would be worth several million dollars.

BOB'S FAILING HEALTH

As the Wailers were gearing up for the American leg of the *Uprising* tour, there was increasing worry and discussion about Bob's health. The reggae superstar was even slimmer than he always had been, and his features were drawn and gaunt. Members of the band blamed this on the busy European touring schedule as they all had their own maladies or ailments coming off the tour.

In September 1980, the band began the American *Uprising* tour in Massachusetts then headed to Rhode Island and New York. The New York shows were held at Madison Square Garden as a supporting act to the American group the Commodores (Lionel Richie's original band). Even after two months of down time, Bob still appeared sick. Not one to talk about his health, Bob brushed off any attempts by members of the band to discuss how he felt. Only once did he tip his hand when he mentioned to his guitarist Al Anderson that his stomach and throat hurt. His voice was thin and hoarse, and rumors began to swirl about suspected drug use (that is, other then the large quantities of ganja that he regularly smoked).

As the Wailers moved through their first American shows of the *Uprising* tour, Bob's health was beginning to visibly fail. In New York, on September 18, the Wailers band moved into the Gramercy Hotel, but Bob stayed at the Essex House away from the group. This isolation was not specifically a cause for alarm, as once in a while Bob stayed at a location away from the band to give him a place in which to conduct interviews and band business. On September 19, Bob sat for several radio interviews and made an appearance at the Jamaican Progressive League. Next he went to Madison Square Garden to prepare the group's sound check.

The Wailers' sound check was postponed because the road crew was still building the Commodores' stage. To Bob's dismay, this postponement eventually turned into an outright cancellation. When the Wailers took the stage that night in front of 20,000 excited fans, their road engineer had to arrange a decent mix while the band was moving through its actual set. The Wailers played their two-night stand at Madison Square Garden in support of the Commodores. After the second show, Bob was bedridden. The exertion of being on stage for the past two nights had left him completely drained and again his health was questioned.

Even though Bob was completely worn out, the tour continued on around him. Rita called him to see if he would be interested in going to an Ethiopian Orthodox Church, but he could not be raised out to bed to go anywhere. Shortly, though, Bob felt well enough to take Alan "Skill" Cole up on an offer to go for a jog in Central Park. While jogging through the park Bob had a seizure and called out to Cole. He collapsed into Cole's arms, unable to move, so Cole carried him back to the hotel. After resting for a while, Bob regained his ability to move, but still did not feel well.

The Wailers: (from left) Bunny, Bob, Carlie, Peter, and Aston ca. 1971. Courtesy of Photofest.

Bob on stage wearing his signature denim shirt in 1976. Courtesy of Photofest.

Bob in the hospital after being shot in 1976. Courtesy of Photofest.

Bob in a contemplative mood in 1978. Courtesy of Photofest.

The Wailers in 1980. Courtesy of Photofest.

Bob on stage in 1980. Courtesy of Photofest.

Bob on stage in 1980 with his Gibson Les Paul guitar. Courtesy of Photofest.

Chapter 5

HOME TO MOUNT ZION

After his collapse in Central Park, Bob rested for several hours. He was immediately joined by Rita and together they tried to reason out what was wrong with him. Bob deflected Rita's fears saying that he was feeling better and just needed to rest. Feeling assured that Bob was going to be all right, Rita agreed to meet him later at a local dance club. The club, called Negril, was located in Greenwich Village, and while Rita and the other I-Threes were there they were told that Bob was not feeling well enough to join them. Bob's health had again taken a turn for the worse.

BOB AND CANCER

The next week dawned with plans to travel to Pittsburgh for the September 23 show at the Stanley Theater. Rita phoned Bob to meet him and ride to the airport together. Bob told her that he would meet her in Pittsburgh as he still had another interview to do in New York. As it turned out, there was no other interview. Bob, concerned about his worsening health, contacted his personal physician, Dr. Frazier, and went to have a checkup. Bob submitted to a variety of X-rays and a brain scan. The results of the tests stopped Bob in his tracks. The doctor's diagnosis was that Bob had a large cancerous brain tumor. Further, the seizure he had had in Central Park had in fact been a stroke.

The doctor directed Bob to cancel the remaining tour dates and immediately submit to cancer treatment. The worst of the grim news was the doctor's prediction that Bob had only two or three weeks left to live. In his typically defiant manner, Bob met this terrible news by saying that he wanted a second opinion. He then made plans to meet the tour in Pittsburgh. Arriving at the Wailers' hotel in Pittsburgh, Bob was met by Rita. Able to read the situation in Bob's face, Rita attempted to cancel the tour on the spot. However, sick or not, Bob was still the leader of the group and would not hear of a cancellation.

On September 23, 1980, Bob Marley and the Wailers performed their final live show. Staged at the Stanley Theater, a medium-sized yet intimate venue that has subsequently been renamed the Benedum Center after substantial renovations. The night of the show, Bob came on stage and without hesitation tore into an incredible set including "Natural Mystic," "Positive Vibration," "Burnin' and Lootin'," "Them Belly Full," "Heathen," and "Running Away/Crazy Baldheads." As part of the Wailers' 90-minute set, the Barrett Brothers moved the rhythms of the songs along at a faster than ordinary pace. Although deathly ill, Bob gave his traditionally energetic performance, following the opening numbers with "War/No More Trouble," "Zimbabwe," "Zion Train," "No Woman, No Cry," "Jamming," and "Exodus." The crowed erupted in applause at the end of the standard set. The Wailers then broke into a series of encores. Typically, Bob did not entertain four encores, but he stayed on stage as long as he could this night.

The first encore was performed by Bob alone, with only his guitar to accompany him. His performance of "Redemption Song" was rendered more poignant with the knowledge that this was his final show. After this solo performance, the rest of the Wailers retook the stage and the second encore was a performance of "Coming In from the Cold." The end of this song should have been the end of the concert. However, Bob motioned to the band to stay on stage and tore into "Is This Love." The final song of the night was the Wailers classic "Work." Constructed as an old-fashioned counting song (counting down instead of up), the performance of this song was Bob marking the end of the band. As he sang "five days to go, working for the next day, four days to go now, working for the next day," the members of the band realized that their leader was counting down to the end of the band. With this the concert ended, and Bob Marley and the Wailers left the stage for the final time.

In the wake of the Pittsburgh show, the rest of the *Uprising* tour was canceled and the Wailers' touring machine was dismantled. The group and entourage refocused their energies from performing to caring for and about Bob. With Rita, Bob went to his mother's house in Miami to consider the next move. Bob wanted to pursue a second opinion and to that end he submitted to additional testing at Cedars of Lebanon Hospital. The doctors at Cedars referred him to the Memorial Sloan-Kettering Cancer

Center in New York. In early October, Bob was tested by the experts at Sloan-Kettering. Bob's hopes were that the original diagnosis would turn out to be incorrect. Instead, he quickly learned that his condition was even worse than originally reported. He not only had a cancerous tumor in his brain, but he also had cancer in his lungs and stomach.

MORE BAD NEWS

With this more specific diagnosis, Bob was informed that he likely had between four and five weeks left to live and that he should put his affairs in order. As a means of relieving the pressure caused by the tumor in his skull, Bob began receiving radiation treatments to try to reduce the size of the brain tumor. An unfortunate result of the Sloan-Kettering visit was that Bob's condition was leaked to the media. On October 8, 1980, news of Bob's cancer was announced on various radio stations in New York. Station WLIB was the first to announce Bob's health concerns over the radio. The news spread quickly and soon Bob's condition was known internationally.

In order to be near to his place of treatment, Bob took up residence in New York. He checked into the historic Wellington Hotel. The hotel's central location, just a few blocks south of Central Park, allowed Bob easy access to his outpatient treatments as well as to anything else he wished to do. Initially, the radiation treatment that Bob had agreed to was successful in controlling his discomfort and he grew stronger. In fact, Bob felt well enough to attend his friend Muhammad Ali's first comeback fight against Larry Holmes. The fight was billed as the "Last Hurrah" and Ali fought valiantly, but at almost 39 years old, he was beaten by a technical knockout by the much younger Holmes, who was in his prime and had been champion for over two years. Bob also attended the New York performance of the rock band Queen, which was touring in support of its 1980 album *The Game*.

At times, Bob even felt well enough to return to his favorite pastime, soccer. He and Cole attempted to play, but Bob soon realized that he was not strong enough to run and he could only sit on the sideline and watch. Although Bob was pushing himself and generally feeling better, he took a turn for the worse when he had another minor stroke. With the toll that this took on his body, Bob was no longer able to stand without assistance and he began to lose weight. Seeing this, Bob's doctors began administering chemotherapy. An unfortunate outcome of this treatment was that Bob's lengthy dreadlocks began to fall out. When this began, Bob requested scissors to cut the rest of his locks and resigned himself to the loss of this signature characteristic. As the chemotherapy progressed, Bob continued to lose weight and he took on an ashen appearance that seemed to signal that the end was near.

BAPTISM INTO THE ETHIOPIAN ORTHODOX CHURCH

Realizing her son's closeness to death, Cedella began pressuring Bob to be baptized into the Ethiopian Orthodox church. At first Bob resisted as he professed his faith to Haile Selassie. However, Cedella reminded Bob that she had been so baptized while Bob was in utero. Bob continued his protest, noting that his affiliation with the Twelve Tribes made him a natural rival of the Ethiopian Orthodox followers. Despite this argument, Bob eventually agreed to be baptized and on November 4, 1980, Bob became a member of the Ethiopian Orthodox church. With this move, Robert Nesta Marley was christened Berhane Selassie. Bob's new name meant "Light of the Holy Trinity." Even as Bob's spirituality grew, his health continued to decline. As a result of the cancer and strokes he was now paralyzed from the waist down and was still losing weight. It began to seem that the chemotherapy itself was hastening Bob's death.

BOB AND UNCONVENTIONAL CANCER TREATMENT

Realizing that the current course of action was not going to allow Bob to live much longer, Bob's physician referred him to a German doctor named Josef Issels. Issels was known for his success with holistic cancer treatment. Although he had been blacklisted by the American Cancer Society, his unconventional methods could do no greater harm to Bob than the cancer was already doing. Feeling as though there was little left to lose, Bob, Cole, and Dr. Frazier engaged Dr. Issels as Bob's physician of last resort.

In early November, Bob and a small group of supporters traveled to Bad Wiessee, Germany. There they located Issels' clinic, called Sunshine House, standing in the shadow of the Bavarian Alps. Bob's condition upon arrival was so poor that there was concern that the trip itself could lead to his death. Reaching Sunshine House, there was speculation that Bob would only live for a few more days. Issels immediately began treating Bob. An important aspect of the treatment was to gain the trust of the wily Rasta.

Gradually, Issels gained Bob's trust and the doctor set about several tasks. First, he had to stabilize Bob's quickly deteriorating condition and then he could work to control the cancer. The initial step was to confirm Bob's earlier diagnosis. Once Issels took an accounting of the cancer in Bob's head, lungs, and stomach, he began treating these afflicted areas. Issels' unorthodox treatments involved hyperthermia, blood transfusions, and injections of THX. Hyperthermia was artificially raising the patient's temperature to heights that the body normally did not have to withstand. Blood transfusions were used to cleanse the weak and overworked cells from the patient's body. The use of THX was not available to Bob in the United States as this drug was not cleared for use in the county. Interestingly nearly 30 years later, THX has still not been proven to have any positive objective effect on cancer. However, Bob's condition began to improve under Issels' care and treatment.

Remarkably, Bob's health continued to improve over the next several weeks. During this period, he and his mother lived at Sunshine House in a small apartment. As his condition improved, Bob was again able to walk short distances. His daily routine included two short walks to his treatment sessions. For treatment, Dr. Issels continued to use hyperthermia sessions, which involved shooting 180-degree beams of ultraviolet heat at Bob's various tumors. The idea behind this type of treatment was that the extreme heat would weaken the cancer cells and allow Bob's own immune system to fight them more effectively. The treatments were long, frequent, and painful, but through it all the noble Rasta endured in silence.

Three months into his treatment, and significantly past when he was originally expected to die, Bob celebrated his 36th birthday. On February 6, 1981, Bob entertained many of the Wailers band members at a birthday celebration in Bad Wiessee. All of the members of the band attended, with the notable exception of the Barrett brothers. Bob's well-wishers had expected to find their former leader near death. Instead, they were greeted by Bob in high spirits, at least passable health, and with some returning hair. A by-product of this gathering was that Bob again became part of the Tuff Gong International machine. Through correspondence with his lawyer, Diane Jobson, Bob began again overseeing the work of his business. This flurry of activity seemed to add to Bob's strength, to the point that he began to engage in light exercise again. Even with this improvement, Jobson noted that Bob weighed only about 100 pounds at his birthday party.

While Bob's early February health was encouraging, by the end of March his mother again noticed his condition worsening. His strength was quickly lost and his ability to walk unassisted went with it Cedella was no longer able to raise her son from long hours of lying in bed. Another discouraging sign came with Bob's refusal to eat or drink. With this, Cedella knew that Bob was not long for this world. Helpless to positively affect her son's health, she instead worked on raising his spirits. To this end, Cedella spent time singing to Bob, reminding him of their good times together in the Jamaican hills and Kingston.

Astonishingly, Dr. Issels choose this pivotal time to take a vacation. Cedella was amazed at the doctor's cavalier attitude to her ailing son's health. Issels left Cedella and Bob in the hands of his assistants in early April. At this point, Bob was a mere shell of his former self. His weight was estimated at just over 70 pounds and he could not care for himself in any meaningful manner. Bob's lawyer Jobson protested the doctor's decision to leave at this time, but to no avail.

Making a bad situation worse was Bob's financial situation. It was common knowledge that he did not have a will and everyone increasingly believed that he could not live much longer. Further compounding these problems, members of the Wailers were making overseas calls pleading for their shares of the band's earnings. Without a will, all of Bob's earnings, future royalties, and song licenses would pass to Rita on his death.

BOB'S RETURN TO MIAMI

Late in April, Dr. Issels returned to Sunshine House and decided to perform surgery on Bob to relieve the pain that the tumor in his stomach was causing. Bob's Rastafarian convictions were again aroused (in opposition to the invasiveness of surgery). However, Bob's condition was so poor that there was little choice. In early May, Bob's doctor admitted to Cedella and Jobson that the most famous Wailer would likely die within the next two weeks. Issels had lost hope in his own treatments to assist Bob any further. In response to this news, it was decided that Bob should be brought back to the home that he had purchased for his mother in Miami. Plans were made quickly to ensure that Bob was strong enough to make the trip. A plane was chartered and the small group made the trip back to the United States. Unable to care for Bob themselves, Cedella and Jobson checked him back into the Cedars of Lebanon Hospital. The staff was not instructed to treat Bob's now numerous afflictions; instead they were simply meant to keep him comfortable in his final days.

Bob survived the transatlantic trip, but continued to weaken. On May 11, 1981, his vital signs became erratic and Rita was summoned. She was told that Bob would likely only live for a few more hours and she should be with him. Rita sat with Bob and sang hymns that she knew he would enjoy. Soon, Bob's breathing became labored and Rita called for Cedella to come and be with her son. By the time she arrived, Bob's condition had stabilized. Cedella and Rita prayed over Bob and he said that he was feeling a little better. During this short rally, Bob said goodbye to his sons Ziggy and Stephen. He also said that he was thirsty. Cedella gave Bob a glass of water, which he drank completely.

Shortly before noon, the nurses had Cedella help them roll Bob onto his side for an X-ray. Afterward, Bob slept for a short time. When he awoke he asked his mother to come close to him. As she did, he lost consciousness briefly and he quietly slipped away. At approximately 11:45 on Wednesday, March 11, 1981, the incendiary voice of the international reggae superstar Robert Nesta Marley was silenced for the final time.

BOB'S FUNERAL ARRANGEMENTS

Bob was memorialized in a service held at his mother's Vista Lane house in Miami the following day. The entire day friends of Bob's streamed through the house, including Sims, Taylor, Blackwell, and various musicians who had played with Bob. Bob's body was on display throughout the day. He was laid in a bronze casket that showed his body from the waist up. In his right hand was a copy of the Bible opened to the Twenty-Third Psalm, and his left hand rested on his favorite guitar. The use of the Twenty-Third Psalm was intentional, as this biblical passage proclaimed that the Lord is the shepherd and that those who dwell in the house of the Lord should fear no evil.

Next, Bob's body was returned to Jamaica for a national funeral. On Tuesday, May 19, Bob's body was brought back to Jamaica for a two-day state funeral arranged by the office of the prime minister. In 1981, Edward Seaga was the prime minister, and Seaga's office arranged for Bob to receive Jamaica's third highest award, the Jamaican Order of Merit. Bob was posthumously granted this award and the associated medal that reads, "He that does the truth comes into the light." The award was presented to Bob's eldest son, Ziggy, on Bob's behalf. With this, Bob became the Honorable Robert Nesta Marley, O.M. Seaga also made May 20 a national day of mourning and Bob's body lay in state. Throughout the day, the coffin was on display for mourners to pay their respects.

Due to Bob's enormous popularity, his body was on display in the National Arena all of Friday, May 20. This allowed even more mourners to view his remains and reports indicate that as many as 40,000 Jamaicans passed through the gates of the arena during the day. As the crowd grew and became uncontrollable, the police unleashed tear gas on the mourners. During the chaos, Bob's body was guarded by the Jamaican police and members of the Twelve Tribes of Israel Rastafarian sect.

In light of his conversion to the Ethiopian Orthodox Church, the following day Bob's body was brought to that church's headquarters on Maxfield Avenue. There Bob's body received the traditional Ethiopian Orthodox funeral. From Maxfield Avenue, Bob's body was taken by motorcade past his house on Hope Road on its way back to the National Arena. A public service was held, including a performance by many of the Wailers. A notable omission was Tyrone Downie, who was too overwhelmed emotionally to perform. Bob's mother, his half-sister Pearl Livingston, and a friend of the family sang a song called "Hail," which was written by Bob's mother. The I-Threes then sang "Rastaman Chant" and "Natural Mystic" with the support of the Wailers.

The public funeral service led by Archbishop Yesuhaq began at 11:00. Yesuhaq was the Ethiopian Orthodox official who had baptized Bob the previous year. The funeral party included Bob's immediate family, Governor-General Florizel Glasspole, and former Jamaican Prime Minster Michael Manley, Alan "Skill" Cole." Glasspole, Manley, and Cole each read biblical passages as assigned by Yesuhaq. Cole read lines from Isaiah and shouted to members of the Twelve Tribes who were in attendance and he thought were being ignored. The archbishop read form Matthew 5 and then all in attendance rose to their feet for the Lord's Prayer. The final speaker was Prime Mister Edward Seaga, who delivered Bob's eulogy. Seaga's words and sentiments were particularly poignant as he and Bob had opposite views on how to run Jamaica. Regardless of their differences, Seaga spoke the following words:

> His message was a protest against injustice, a comfort for the oppressed. He stood there, performed there, his message reached there and everywhere. Today's funeral service is an international right of a native son. He was born in a humble cottage nine miles from Alexandria in the parish of St. Ann. He lived in the western section of Kingston as a boy where he joined in the struggle of the ghetto. He learned the message of survival in his boyhood days in Kingston's west end. But it was his raw talent, unswerving discipline and sheer perseverance that transported him from just another victim of the ghetto to the top ranking superstar in the entertainment industry of the third world.

After Seaga's eulogy, Bob's casket was loaded into the open back of a blue and white Chevrolet pickup truck by a military detail of six men clothed in white coats with black belts and black pants. A blue blanket was tacked to the top of the truck's bed to shade the casket from the sun. As Bob began his last journey to his ancestral home in Nine Mile, nyabinghi hand drummers played as he went. The truck was followed for a short time by a robed priest with incense. The long motorcade began winding its way from Kingston to St. Ann's parish. On the 55-mile route, Bob's body passed thousands of Jamaicans on hand to bid their national hero a fond farewell. Along the way, Bob's body passed over the Blue Mountains and was witnessed by a seemingly constant stream of people along the sides of the road.

When the motorcade reached Nine Mile it was greeted by another teaming horde of well-wishers. Five hours after leaving Kingston, Bob's body was finally coming to its last resting place. On the grounds of Bob's familial homestead, a modest white mausoleum had been built. Bob's body was enshrined within this single-chamber tomb within sight of where he had been born. The tomb itself was blessed by officials of the Twelve Tribes and the Ethiopian Orthodox Church. In the presence of his family and many onlookers, Bob's tomb was sealed three times. The first seal was a red metal plate with a gold Star of David, the second was a metal grate that was bolted on, and the third was a layer of free concrete that was patted into place by several Rastafarians with their bare hands.

Bob was laid to rest with the kind of pomp and circumstance that was only afforded to heads of state. During the funeral and the ride across the island, it was estimated that his motorcade was viewed by in excess of one hundred thousand people. Since his enshrinement, Bob's patriarchal home has become a place of pilgrimage, to which people travel from all over the world to visit the fallen reggae warrior's remains.

Chapter 6

THE LEGACY AND THE LEGEND

Bob received many significant rewards during his abbreviated life. Two of the most significant were the 1976 *Rolling Stone Magazine* award for Band of the Year and the 1978 Peace Medal of the Third World from the United Nations. However, in death, praise was virtually heaped upon the reggae superstar. These awards are a testament to Bob's legacy and illustrate the strength and influence of his musical style. In 1994, Bob was inducted into the Rock and Roll Hall of Fame in Cleveland, Ohio. With this he joined a small and elite group of American music superstars. Since it opened its doors in 1993, the Rock and Roll Hall of Fame has inducted only 97 members and Bob Marley is one of them.

Bob has also been honored by receiving the 43rd Grammy Lifetime Achievement Award. He has his own star on the Hollywood Walk of Fame, and in 1999 his album *Exodus* was recognized by *Time* magazine as the Album of the Century. The British Broadcasting Company (BBC) named Bob's song "One Love" their Song of the Millennium. In 2004, *Rolling Stone Magazine* ranked him #11 on their list of the 100 Greatest Artists of All Time. Also, the BBC has recognized him as one of the greatest lyricists of all time. The Jamaican government annually bestows a Bob Marley Award for Culture, and the Caribbean Music Expo presents a Bob Marley Lifetime Achievement award each year. Possibly his highest honor is that since his death Bob has sold in excess of 21.3 million albums. For greater clarity on this figure, one must understand that such sales were not even counted until 1991, when SoundScan became a reliable entity.

Another distinct and seldom bestowed honor was awarded to Bob after his death. In 2002, the Gibson guitar company began issuing a limited edition Bob Marley Les Paul special guitar. The Les Paul series guitar was Bob's favorite electric guitar for use on stage and in the studio. As a memento of the label's appreciation of Bob's long association with the Gibson brand, the legendary guitar maker joined forces with the legendary reggae musician. The Marley Gibson Special was built to the exact specifications of Bob's Les Paul on display at the Bob Marley Museum. Bob had modified his Les Paul in a few important ways, and Gibson duplicated these characteristics in the signature series guitar. The initial run of the Bob Marley Les Paul Special was limited to 200 guitars.

POSTHUMOUS RELEASES

Bob's life after death has had almost as much activity and interest associated with it as did his mortal life. When Bob died, he left behind a prodigious library of recordings; however, there was also a large number of unreleased songs that have continued to surface. Some of the more important posthumous releases included *Legend, Confrontation, Chances Are, Africa Unite: The Single Collection, Talkin' Blues, Songs of Freedom, Natural Mystic, the Legend Lives On: Bob Marley and the Wailers*, and the Deluxe Edition re-releases.

CHANCES ARE AND *CONFRONTATION*

In 1981, Danny Simms released the nine-song album *Chances Are*. This record contained previously unreleased material and new versions of previously released material. In 1983, Tuff Gong International and Island Records released *Confrontation*. This album was conceived of by Bob toward the end of his life. He recorded the tracks during the *Uprising* sessions and had his hand in all parts of making this release, except choosing the specific songs included and the order they appeared in. Rita stepped in to make these decisions.

The album was a testament to Bob's career. The album cover depicts the reggae superstar riding a white horse slaying a dragon with a lance in the traditional mold of St. George. The back of the jacket included a painting of the first battle between the Ethiopians and the Italians. Called the Battle of Adowa, this 1896 battle foreshadowed the fighting that eventually drove Haile Selassie into exile. The album contained the songs "Chant Down Babylon," "Buffalo Soldier," "Jump Nyabinghi," "Mix Up, Mix Up," "Give Thanks and Praises," "Blackman Redemption," "Trench Town," "Stiff Necked Fools," "I Know," and "Rastaman Live Up." The songs represent an excellent cross section of Bob's writing at the apex of his abilities.

LEGEND

The next major title released under Bob's name was titled *Legend*. Released in 1984, the album was subtitled *The Best of Bob Marley*. However, due to the sheer quantity of Bob's song output, 14 songs could not complete the proposed purpose. However, the album did an admirable job of presenting a picture of Bob's output over the course of his career. In typical Wailers fashion, the remaining members of the group prepared a tour in support of the album. Downie and Marvin shared the singing duties and Ziggy joined the tour to lead the group for the Los Angeles show. *Legend* spent over two years on the American Top 200 Albums charts and it was on the UK charts for 129 weeks. Incredibly, the album spent just over 11 years on Billboard's Top Pop Catalogue Album chart. This album went on to become the best-selling reggae release of all time and has been certified platinum 10 times. As of 2006, *Legend* had sold in excess of 12 million copies and continues to sell at a brisk pace.

SONGS OF FREEDOM

Another important release was the 1992 four-CD boxed set *Bob Marley: Songs of Freedom*. An officially licensed product of Tuff Gong and Island Records, the original pressing of this set was limited to one million copies. In 1999 there was a second pressing in a slightly different format, which did not change the fact that this was the definitive collection of Bob's songs, spanning his entire career. The release began with several of Bob's earliest singles and came forward in time to the acoustic version of "Redemption Song."

THE SINGLES COLLECTION

Africa Unite: The Singles Collection was released in November 2005. Unlike many of the other posthumous releases, this album had a defined purpose and deliberate design. Released for Bob's 60th birthday celebration, the collection revels in much of Bob's most outstanding material. The album was unique in that it contained material that spanned Bob's career in addition to including two hip-hop remixes and a previously unreleased track. The final three tracks were the most significant on the release, as they were not available elsewhere.

Will.i.am, a member of the American hip-hop group the Black Eyed Peas, was responsible for the remixing of "Africa Unite." Completed in December 2004, the song took on a new life in the hands of a contemporary producer/songwriter. The Black Eyed Peas added a stronger beat presence, additional instrumental textures, echoes on some vocals, and new words sung by Will himself. Overall, the remix clocked in at twice the original song's length and received a hip-hop generation upgrade that brought in into the new millennium.

The other remix was really a contemporary mashup. The idea of a mashup song is taking two existing songs and combining them in a manner that creates a third song that is a hybrid of the first two. Here the English DJ Ashley Beedle mashed together Bob's fire-and-brimstone classic "Get Up, Stand Up" and Bob's son Damian's hot 2005 single "Welcome to Jamrock." The combined version of the song began with the DJ reversing a record and then the beat from "Jamrock" dropped. However, instead of staying with Damian's words, the DJ superimposed Bob's words. An especially interesting twist was the insertion of the word "Jamrock" at the end of each phrase of Bob's lyrics. An additional treat was the presence of Peter Tosh. Tosh sang the second verse in the original song and that performance was repeated here (although only in recording: Tosh has been dead since 1987). With this song, Bob's message was again updated for the hip-hop generation, but this time passed through the lens of his own son's song.

The only truly previously unreleased song on the album was titled "Slogans." The song was originally recorded in 1979 while Bob was in Miami. The original tape of the song was found in Cedella's house, and consisted of little more than vocals and a drum machine beat. Bob's sons Ziggy and Stephen took the raw tape material and built the rest of the song. They added instrumental lines that complete the texture and the final product sounds much like other material completed by their father. The two Marley sons enlisted the assistance of the rock guitar legend Eric Clapton to supply the lead guitar lines. The message of the song was still as important in 2005 as it was in 1979. Bob sang of his contempt for the constant propagandizing of the Catholic Church and the Jamaican government. The slogans that he referred to were those empty promises made from the pulpit of the church and the grandstand of the political rally.

THE DELUXE EDITIONS

Another series of releases that have come out after Bob's death and are exemplary in quality and detail are the Deluxe Editions. Island and Tuff Gong records began re-releasing the classic Wailers' material in 2001 and, thus far, have issued *Catch a Fire, Exodus, Legend, Rastaman Vibration,* and *Burnin'*. These re-releases are unique in that they all contain the original album material in remastered clarity by producer Dill Levenson. The second CD of each set differs from one release to the next. For *Catch a Fire*, released in 2001, the second CD contained the previously unreleased Jamaican versions of the songs that appeared on the original album. Additional songs on the first CD included versions of "High Tide or Low Tide" and "All Day, All Night."

The *Exodus* Deluxe Edition was also released in 2001. Again, the first disc contained the remastered versions of the original songs. However, in this case, Levenson added five alternate songs and versions of "Roots," "Waiting in Vain," "Jamming," "Jamming (long version)," and "Exodus." The second disc contained a combination of studio and live cuts. The studio offerings were recorded and produced by Lee "Scratch" Perry. Studio songs on disc two included two versions of "Punky Reggae Party," two cover versions of the Curtis Mayfield song "Keep On Moving," and "Exodus." The live songs were recorded at the Rainbow Theater show of the *Exodus* tour on June 4, 1977. Included were "The Heathen," "Crazy Baldhead," "War/No More Trouble," "Jamming," and "Exodus."

The next Deluxe Edition came out in 2002 with the re-release of *Rastaman Vibration*. Again the first disc of the two-CD set contained the remastered versions of the songs on the original album. To this Levenson added eight additional songs recorded in Kingston or London at the same time as the original material was recorded. The second disc contained live performances from the Wailers May 26, 1976, show at the Roxy Theatre. Recorded during the *Rastaman Vibration* tour, the live material was an excellent testament to the quality and potency that Bob had achieved with this band. Additional tracks on the second disc of this set were two versions of the song "Smile Jamaica," one labeled part one and the other labeled part two.

The Deluxe Edition of *Legend* was also released in 2002. The first disc of digitally remastered tracks was accompanied by a second disc containing alternate versions of the original 16 songs. These versions were collected from remixing sessions dating from 1980 to 1984. The producers that remixed the material on the second disc include Paul "Graucho" Smykle, Errol Brown, Alex Sadkin, and Eric "E.T." Thorngren. In keeping with the original release of this album, the *Legend* Deluxe Edition has been a consumer favorite.

The most recent Deluxe Edition was released in 2004. The *Burnin'* installment in this series contained the remastered tracks on the first disc with the addition of five songs produced at the time of the original sessions, but omitted at the time. Because *Burnin'* was such an early album, two of the additional songs were written by other members of the original

Wailers trio. "No Sympathy" was written by Peter Tosh and Bunny Wailer wrote "Reincarnated Souls." The second disc included a 12-song live set. The live tracks were recorded via the Island mobile studio at the Leeds show on November 23, 1973. All of the versions on this disc were previously unreleased and represent the Wailers during their transitional phase after Peter and Bunny left the group.

Although Bob has been dead for over 25 years, posthumous releases from the artist continue. The reggae superstar's catalog is now several times the size it was at his passing and shows few signs of slowing down. Imports, bootlegs, live shows, and various types of compilations surface progressively. In 2006 alone there were more than 12 full-length releases in Marley's name. The market is completely flooded with Bob's material and the commodification of the reggae legend is completely staggering.

BOB'S ESTATE

The topic of money turns to the handling of Bob's business affairs after his death. As mentioned above, Bob died intestate (without a will). This left control of the largest third world music legacy and a multimillion-dollar estate in the hands of his wife Rita. There followed years of nasty legal battles for the proper distribution of royalties, property, and ownership. In the wake of Bob's death, Rita moved the Tuff Gong Recording studios and production offices to 220 Marcus Garvey Drive, Kingston 11. The home offices of the Tuff Gong International are still at this location.

Rita's next step was the conversion of the house at 56 Hope Road into a museum and library where international guests are welcome to take guided tours of the property and house. Bob's former dwelling now hosts thousands of tourists each year. The structure of the house remains unchanged since Bob's passing, but several rooms have been altered to suit their specific purposes. The upstairs bedrooms have been converted into gallery space that contains a world map with all of Bob's concert tour performance locations marked with colored thumb tacks. The second-story room that was once Ziggy's bedroom has been converted into a makeshift business office and library. Here, books and newspaper articles about Bob and the Wailers are preserved and made available to investigators.

Bob's upstairs master bedroom remains in the same condition as it was when he last slept there. Although Bob was a very public person, this space gives tour participants a glimpse into the more private side of the man. The main floor of the house contains part of the original Tuff Gong recording studios. The studios remain in working order and are still in occasional use. Of particular interest is the kitchen. Preserved since the mid-1970s, the kitchen at the back of the house still exhibits the holes in the walls created by the bullets sprayed into the room during the 1976 assassination attempt.

The grounds around the house at 56 Hope Road are now quite crowded. During Bob's life, these grounds were used for parking spaces and as a soccer field. Now the grounds are covered with a variety of tourist attractions. At the edge of the yard is Rita's Queen of Sheba Restaurant, where traditional Ital food and fruit drinks are served. Behind the house, where there used to be rehearsal space, there is now a newer building used to house the Bob Marley Theatre. Along the side of the property is another relatively new building that houses the Things from Africa Boutique.

Beyond the management of the property at 56 Hope Road, Rita suffered from lack of experience when handling Bob's estate. Trouble arose with virtually every facet of the management of Bob's vast empire. Money was misappropriated, relationships with members of the Wailers band were tarnished, and a great deal of time and money was spent trying to figure everything out. One serious misstep was taken in 1986, when the remaining members of the Wailers band were essentially forced into signing away their rights to future royalties for a flat fee. The amounts of money ended up being pennies on the dollars of the future, but were immediate payoffs.

In 1987, Rita's handling of the Marley estate again took a turn for the worse. Rita, her accountant Martin Zolt, and her lawyer David Steinberg were collectively accused of fraud. Rumors had been swirling around Jamaica that Rita was hiding money in the Caymans and thus separating Bob's estate into taxable and untaxed income. At this point, Rita was taken out of the management role and replaced by a court-appointed bank administrator. This led to many problems in the Marley family, as their collective assets were frozen and even Cedella's house in Miami was temporarily seized.

THE LEGAL BATTLE

The details of much of the early proceedings from Rita, Zolt, and Steinberg's trial are murky. However, it was found that the trio was guilty of fraud, breach of fiduciary duty, and violations of the Racketeer Influenced and Corrupt Organizations Act (RICO). Because Bob died intestate, Jamaican law ruled that Rita was responsible for 10 percent of his estate outright, plus 45 percent held as a life interest. Bob's 11 children were each entitled to equal shares of the remaining 45 percent outright, plus a remainder interest in Rita's 45 percent life estate.

Also discovered during these initial proceedings was the fact that from 1981 to 1986, those controlling Bob's estate implemented several schemes that allegedly diverted foreign music assets and royalty income away from Bob's estate and into accounts held outside the estate. Rita, Zolt, and Steinberg protested, saying that these diverted funds were used to establish new corporations for the purposes of minimizing tax liability and leaving more money for Bob's beneficiaries. Lawyers for the State named at least four schemes and produced signed documents proving the collusion of the three implicated in the suit. In short, Rita and her representatives were not reporting the majority of the royalties that Bob's music was earning.

For a time, lawsuits, deceit, and chaos overshadowed Bob's musical legacy. The end result of these legal machinations was that the Bob Marley estate was put up for sale as a unit by the Jamaican government. Chris Blackwell, Bob's longtime friend and record company boss, purchased the ownership of the estate for the minuscule sum of 8.6 million dollars. Blackwell's company, Island Logic Inc., was successful in the auction for Bob's estate against the opposition of members of Bob's own family. For 8.6 million dollars, Blackwell gained the rights to all of Bob's songs, his recordings, and his future royalties. Subsequently, Blackwell sold the rights to Bob's catalogue to the German record company Polygram in 1989. Polygram was absorbed by Seagrams in 1998, and the new music collective was named the Universal Music Group. Thus, Bob's music changed hands yet again.

Even through all of the legal difficulties and troubles with defining ownership, Bob's legacy persisted. Although the initial licensing was lost, Bob's family has remained well off financially, as they control all other aspects of his output. Also, unreleased material was not covered by the original court arrangement and through the surfacing of many additional versions and studio outtakes; much of Bob's music is again controlled by his family. Regardless of where the ownership of Bob's music lies, in his own words, his truest legacy was in his children.

Chapter 7

THE MARLEY FAMILY

The two remaining matriarchs of the Marley family are the principal keepers of the family legacy. Bob's mother Cedella and wife Rita continue to carry on Bob's work even more than 25 years after his death. Although Cedella was not always active in Bob's career during his life, she has become quite active after his death. As the oldest member of the Marley family, she is the protector of his legacy.

CEDELLA MARLEY BOOKER

Cedella Marley Booker (born July 23, 1926) still lives in the house that Bob bought her in Miami, Florida. She acts as the official matriarch of the family and is still involved in much of the business of the family. She has taken equal care of the children that Bob bore to Rita and his children born outside the marriage. As part of her nurturing of her son's legacy, his mother has released two albums of her own music. In 1991, she issued *Awake Zion* on the RIOR label with the assistance of Bob's old bass player, Aston "Family Man" Barrett. In the following year, she issued her second album, called *Smilin' Island Song*.

Cedella has also written several books on her son's life. She authored the book *Bob Marley: An Intimate Portrait by His Mother* and another book, *Bob Marley My Son*. In addition, mother "Ciddy" has also toured widely, speaking on the importance of her famous son and singing her own songs. Her tours have taken her across the United States, through much of Western Europe, into Africa, around Mexico, and throughout the Caribbean. More recently, she has taken to producing hand-crafted dolls, which are sold though several Web sites.

RITA MARLEY

Rita Marley, born Alpharita Anderson in Cuba in on July 25, 1946, was the other principal leader of the Marley family. After Bob's death, Rita's legal problems mounted and she lost control of the Marley family fortune. However, in the aftermath of this initial loss, Rita was able to support herself and the family and to build a new fortune. One aspect of Rita's furthering of Bob's legacy was the release of her own music. In 1981 she released the album *Who Feels It Knows It*, in 1988 she released *Harambe*, and in 1988 she issued *We Must Carry On*. Rita began her musical career as the leader of her own band, and she returned to front woman form after her years singing backup to Bob.

In the 1990s, Rita again issued a series of albums. These records were on the Shanachie imprint. Among these were *Beauty of God, Good Girls Cult*, and *One Draw*. These were followed by *Sings Bob Marley . . . and Friends, Play Play, Sunshine After Rain*, and *Gifted Fourteen Carnation*, all issued in the new millennium. Rita also released a book on her life with Bob that has the unique perspective of a woman interacting in a very male-dominated scene. The book, called *No Woman, No Cry: My Life with Bob Marley*, was co-authored with Hettie Jones.

Recently, Rita has remained active in the music business largely through the activities of her many children. She is engaged in the furthering and protection of her husband's legacy and attends annual worldwide birthday celebrations concerts in his honor. Rita has also established the Rita Marley Foundation to provide much needed supplies and infrastructural improvements to underdeveloped parts of Africa. The main goal of the group is to provide safe drinking water to the thousands of African people struggling for subsistence.

In January 2005, Rita announced her intention to have Bob's body removed from the mausoleum in Nine Mile and reburied in his spiritual home in Ethiopia. This news came as part of the month-long celebration of Bob's 60th birthday. The move was backed by Ethiopian church and government officials. At the time, Rita asserted that it was part of Bob's mission to return to Africa and the movement of his casket would fulfill the fallen reggae superstar's intentions. Rita proposed to have Bob's body reburied in Shashamani, about 155 miles south of Addis Ababa. Bob had visited this Rastafarian enclave on his first trip to Africa.

Rita's announcement was met with strong disagreement from many Jamaicans. Representatives of the Bob Marley Foundation immediately refuted Rita's claims, saying there were no plans to move Bob. In fact, the news of a possible reburial created such a widespread outcry in opposition that Rita was forced to retract her earlier statement. First Rita said that no decision was yet made, and she eventually moved to the position that Bob's remains would stay in Nine Mile. The uprising about the possible move did create a renewed interest in all things Marley leading up to his 60th birthday celebration, but the concern was that this interest was more negative than positive. Regardless of possible missteps, Rita remains the focal point of the Marley family. She remains quite hands on with the management of the Marley legacy and has taken over the role of mother of all of Bob's children without concern for Bob's extramarital affairs.

During his life, Bob continuously professed his love for children. He included in this not just his own children but the children of the world. With this in mind, one could see Bob's most lasting legacy as his 11 children. Bob's own thoughts on this were captured in his statement that he wanted to have as many children as there were shells on the beach. Regardless of moral codes, Bob fathered three children with Rita and accepted two other children of hers as his own. Bob adopted Rita's daughter Sharon, whose birth father was an unnamed man with whom Rita conceived her daughter prior to her meeting Bob. Rita's daughter Stephanie was also unlikely to have been fathered by Bob. It has been generally accepted that Stephanie's father was a Rasta called Ital. Regardless of who their fathers were, Bob cared for these children as his own.

During their marriage, Bob had several often highly publicized affairs. Many of these affairs yielded children who were eventually accepted, by Rita, into the extended Marley family unit. Other children that Bob fathered were Damian, Rohan, Robbie, Karen, Julian, Ky-Mani, and Makeda Jahnesta. Each child had a unique position in Bob's life and several of his children, both from his marriage to Rita and outside it, continue Bob's musical legacy.

SHARON MARLEY

Although Bob was not the genetic father of Sharon (known as Sharon Marley Prendergrass), he treated her as a daughter throughout his life. He adopted her when he and Rita got married and doted on her constantly. Often described as Bob's "favorite," Sharon has spent her life forwarding many aspects of Bob's vision. From 18 months of age onward, Bob was Sharon's father, and as any good father would do, he attempted to guide her in her life's pursuits. As she was growing up, the Marley household was always filled with music. As Bob's fame grew, Sharon was increasingly aware of life in the music world. However, her father cautioned her against going into music as a profession as he knew first hand how difficult a business it is.

Even with her father's advice ringing in her ears, as an adult Sharon has had several jobs related to the music industry. She has helped to preserve Bob's musical legacy as a member of the Marley children's band, the Melody Makers. She is currently the director of the Bob Marley Museum in Kingston, Jamaica, and she has pursued an acting career as part of the cast of the Denzel Washington/Robert Townshend movie *The Mighty Quinn*. Other aspects of Sharon's professional life include her work with the Caribbean business Ghetto Youths International and her work in attempting to open a day care training center in Jamaica. The center would be the first of its kind on the island and reflects Bob's interest in caring for children.

CEDELLA

The first child born of Bob and Rita's marriage was named Cedella, after Bob's mother. Cedella was born in August 1967 in Kingston and her birth corresponded with the release of the Wailers single. "Nice Time." As a result, she was given the title of the song as a nickname. She grew up in a fairly traditional manner, attending attended public schools. Just as with Sharon, Bob wanted Cedella to become a doctor or a lawyer, but she followed her father's footsteps into music.

Musically, Cedella took a lead role in forming the Marley children's group, the Melody Makers. She is known for her beautiful singing voice and is also a talented dancer. In addition to the Melody Makers, Cedella formed a splinter group called the Marley Girls. Her professional involvement with Bob's legacy centers on her role as the CEO of Tuff Gong International. In addition to her recording, singing, and management of Bob's record label, Cedella finds time to be active in raising her own group of Marley children. Known for her tenacity, Cedella aggressively works to safeguard and develop her father's legacy.

DAVID (ZIGGY)

Sharon and Cedella's next younger sibling is a brother, David, born on October 17, 1968. Although David was his given name, he was almost immediately nicknamed Ziggy and has been known by this name ever since. Again warned against following in his father's musical footsteps, Ziggy was bitten by the musical bug as a youth. He grew up listening to his father's music along with the material of legendary American artists such as Stevie Wonder.

Music industry insiders consider Ziggy the natural heir to his father's musical throne. He shares many of his father's facial features and his voice is similar to Bob's. Also, due to his age, he was able to witness and participate in parts of Bob's musical odyssey. Ziggy was in Zimbabwe with his father for the concert celebrating the freedom of that country. Further, he became the de facto head of the family on his father's passing. As such, he received Bob's Order of Merit on behalf of his father.

As a musician, Ziggy was the musical head of the Melody Makers. This point was made clear when the band began to be known as Ziggy Marley and the Melody Makers. Since his father's death, Ziggy has been on an extended musical odyssey of his own. He worked with the Melody Makers through the release of seven studio albums (and several greatest hits collections) and has pursued a solo career, unlike many of the other Marley children.

The premier Marley children's musical group is the Melody Makers. The group consists of Sharon, Cedella, Ziggy, and Stephen. The group got its formal beginning when the members recorded a song that Bob had written for and about them in 1979, called "Children Playing in the Streets." However, the group had unofficially been formed in 1981 to sing at Bob's funeral. Since its inception, the Melody Makers have consistently put out salable reggae music that preserves their father's legacy. Although the musical product of the group swerves from pop offerings to more serious roots-sounding works, collectively the group's output has been a testament to its members' musical heritage.

Over the course of several decades, the Melody Makers have released several albums. Additionally, they have toured internationally and been part of the Reggae Sunsplash concert series that their father helped start. Their releases began in the mid-1980s with the album *Play the Game Right*. Their second release was 1986's *Hey World!* This was followed by *One Bright Day* in 1988 and *Conscious Party* in 1989. The style of reggae music that the Melody Makers were putting out at this time was inspired by their father's material, but did not sound much like it. However, the Melody Makers' products were commercially viable and of high enough quality that they were in demand as singers and songwriters.

Albums from the group continued to come out in the 1990s. *Jahmekya* was released in 1991 and was followed by *Fallen Is Babylon* in 1997. The 1999 album, *Spirit of Music,* was heralded as a return to conscious reggae roots for the group. Throughout these many releases, the Melody Makers have continued to forward their father's, and by extension reggae music's, cause of bringing conscious music to the masses. Interestingly, after Bob's death, the prevalent type of Jamaican popular music turned way from roots reggae and toward the dancehall style. Dancehall has much more in common with American hip-hop than it does with the social or political themes in conscious reggae. With their music, the Melody Makers continued to blaze the trail started by their father instead of falling in with the new style of the time.

Within this context, Ziggy matured as a singer and songwriter. Taking a page from his father's book of ambition, Ziggy set about the task of writing music that could reach a global audience. As a testament to his success, he has reached that audience and achieved an American Top 40 single. To say that Ziggy got an early start is to state the obvious. He was the natural front person for the Melody Makers with his father's good looks and attractive voice, but he ended up fronting an internationally viable group at the tender age of 17. One might think that following in Bob's footsteps made Ziggy's movement into the music world easy. On the contrary, his father had established astonishingly large shoes to fill and Ziggy's youthful songwriting skills were held up in comparison to Bob's mature work.

Early on, in order to carve out his own niche, Ziggy allowed his music to move more into popular mainstream circles. This resulted in harsh criticism from the roots reggae core; however, it was speculated that the young Marley was simply finding his own voice and separating himself from the enormous pressure of his father's songwriting legacy. Another problem in Ziggy's life at the time was the marked desire of EMI (the Melody Makers' record label) to push Ziggy as a solo artist, instead of the leader of a group of his siblings. This conflict caused the group to switch to the Virgin Records label.

The move to Virgin resulted in their most popular material to date. The songs on *Conscious Party* were a great success for the group. Produced with the assistance of Talking Heads band members Chris Frantz and Tina Weymouth, this release was both commercially and critically acclaimed. The album climbed to number 39 on the American popular music charts and affirmed that the Melody Makers were not just riding on their famous father's coattails.

The 1989 follow-up to *Conscious Party*, titled *One Bright Day*, was another big success for Ziggy and the Melody Makers. The album climbed into the American Top 20 and showed that the previous album had not been a fluke. Both of these late 1980s offerings won the group Grammy Awards for Best Reggae Album of the Year. The early 1990s brought continued success with the release of the *Jahmekya* album. The release sold well and made it into the Top 20; however, it did not have radio-friendly singles, unlike the previous two albums. The follow-up album, *Joy and Blues* of 1993, contained some dancehall style material that featured Stephen. The album did not sell well and marked the group's departure from Virgin Records and their move to Elektra Records.

For Elektra, the group released 1995's *Free Like We Want 2 B*. With this, it seemed that Ziggy and the Melody Makers had regained some of their previous form. In 1997, *Fallen Is Babylon* won the group another Grammy Award and showed that Ziggy's songwriting skills were still in top form. Through the course of these later releases, Ziggy emerged from the group as a soloist. The Melody Makers are still a group in name, but Ziggy had begun to work on individual recording projects.

In addition to his solo work, Ziggy was becoming a leading political voice. He was named a Goodwill Youth Ambassador for the United Nations and spoke publicly on topics of injustice, poverty, and the third world. Additionally, he launched his own record label, called Ghetto Youths United (Ghetto Youth Crew), which he is using to foster the talent of the next generation of reggae artists. His charity work is well known and he has been involved in United Resources Giving Enlightenment (URGE), which performs community service in Jamaica.

In the new millennium, Ziggy continued to emerge as a solo artist and leader of the next generation of Jamaican music. On April 15, 2003, he released his first official solo album, titled *Dragonfly*. The album cover depicts Ziggy with dreadlocks to his waist and a dragonfly on a yellow background. He was credited as the writer and singer for all 11 songs included on the release, which was met with a degree of success. Ziggy followed this up with a second solo release in 2006, called *Love Is My Religion*.

In addition to music, Ziggy has pursued a varied career in the entertainment industry. In 2004, he voiced a Rasta jellyfish in the movie *Shark Tale* and together with Sean Paul created a new version of his father's song "Three Little Birds" for the movie's soundtrack. Ziggy also sang the theme song for the PBS show *Arthur* and continues to come into his own as a soloist. As he ages, his voice becomes more and more like his father's as he grows into a leadership role in the international reggae community.

Like Bob, Ziggy has fathered a significant group of children. With long-time companion Lorraine Bogle, Ziggy has three children, Daniel (a son), Justice (a daughter) and Zouri (a daughter). Ziggy is now married to Orly Agai, with whom he has had several other children. Judah Victoria is their daughter, born on April 7, 2005, and their son Gideon Robert Nesta Marley was born on January 5, 2007. While continuing to pursue his own career, charitable and philanthropic endeavors, and family interests, Ziggy remembers the words of his father: "every man has to stand up for his rights."

STEPHEN

The next Marley child, and Bob's second son, was Stephen, born April 20, 1972. Stephen was born in Wilmington, Delaware, while Rita was living there with Cedella. The youngest member of the Melody Makers, Stephen has become an accomplished singer, DJ, writer, and producer. His earliest recordings were made at age six when he helped lay down the vocal tracks for "Children Playing in the Streets." The song was recorded as a charity endeavor and the proceeds from the single were donated to the United Nations in support of the International Year of the Child. Additionally, Stephen danced and participated in Bob's live shows, spending time on stage. In addition to an early life spent on stage with his father, at age seven Stephen began learning the acoustic guitar.

Because of this early exposure to music, Stephen has been immersed in the art form and has been a professional musician for the majority of his years. In addition to his performing, he has been an integral part of the record label Ghetto Youths United. As a producer, Stephen has made several well-known remixes of his father's work and coupled these with famous living singers such as Lauryn Hill (one of the three members of the Fugees). His work with Hill led to the Melody Makers performance with the Fugees at the 1997 Grammy Awards Show in New York City.

Stephen's production work began in 1996 when he filled the producer role for tracks on albums by his brothers Damian and Julian. His production work has also allowed Stephen to cross styles of music extensively. He has mixed reggae, hip-hop, and rhythm and blues. Work with hip-hop artists such as Krayzie Bones (from Bone Thugs-N-Harmony), Eve (of the hip-hop set the Ruff Ryders), and Erykah Badu has increased his credentials and connected his father's legacy to current styles of music.

As a producer, he worked on his brother Damian's album *Halfway Tree*, released in 2001. The album was a huge success and scored a Grammy for the Best Reggae Album of the Year. His version of Stevie Wonder's Bob Marley tribute song "Master Blaster" was of such quality that it was placed on the 2005 Wonder tribute album, *Conception*. As a songwriter, Stephen has not been as productive as some of his siblings.

He began work on an album in 2002, but this was delayed by his work with the Ghetto Youths International production house. The album was meant to come out in 2006 under the title *Got Music?* Although the tracks were complete, Stephen opted not to release the album. Some speculation circulated that the album was put on hold to avoid conflicting with other Marley family records. Stephen is making 2007's *Mind Control* his first official album-length release. He is currently streaming the album's title track on his Myspace page and hopes are high for a successful, long-anticipated release.

Although in his mid-thirties, Stephen already boasts a nearly three-decade-long career in music. As such, the release of his album has created significant interest. The album blends reggae, rock, rhythm and blues, nyabinghi, flamenco, and hip-hop into a unique and unnamed hybrid. As is customary in contemporary American hip-hop, the *Mind Control* album features various cameo appearances including those of Ben Harper, Mos Def, Damian Marley, Maya Azucena and Illestr8, Spragga Benz, and Mr. Cheeks.

Through the course of his career, Stephen has done wonders to enhance Bob's musical legacy in the area of introducing his father's music to a whole new audience. Stephen is a five-time Grammy winner in his own right and is still at the beginning of what promises to be a long and fruitful career. Stephen's defiant attitude and distaste for underhanded political dealings are present in his lyrics and he puts forward his father's message throughout. To help preserve the legacy, Stephen was part of two American tours in 2006. Most notable was the critically acclaimed Bob Marley Roots, Rock Reggae Festival, which also included his brother Ziggy. This tour placed Stephen on stage with one of his father's oldest friends and one-third of the original Wailers singing trio, Bunny Wailer.

As is true of most of the Marley children, Stephen has children of his own. For a time he was married to Kertie DaCosta and together they had a son, Jeremiah, and a daughter, Sasha. Additionally, he had four other children from various relationships. His other children are sons Joseph, Stephan, and Yohan, and a daughter called Summer. Stephen's current relationship is with fashion designer and singer Kristina Marawski, with whom he recently had a daughter called Zipporah.

STEPHANIE

Another Marley daughter was Stephanie, born in 1974. There are several conflicting reports concerning her lineage. Some say that Bob was her father, and others report that her father was a local Rasta called Ital. Rita reported, in her book *No Woman No Cry: My Life with Bob Marley*, that Stephanie's father was probably Bob. However, at this time, Rita and Bob were not getting along and Rita had entered into a relationship with a local Rasta called Tacky. This local Rasta called Tacky was, in fact, the Jamaican soccer star Owen Stewart. In the account in her book, Rita was very careful never to say that she and Tacky had had a sexual relationship; however, it was implied.

Regardless of who her biological father was, Stephanie was born on August 17, 1974, and Bob was her father to all intents and purposes. She grew up in Kingston and was educated in Jamaican primary and secondary schools. She moved to England and completed her A-level studies in psychology and social studies in London. Next, Stephanie studied psychology at the University of Western Ontario, Canada. She earned her bachelor's degree with honors and during her studies she was active with local children's groups. She paid extra attention to children with special needs.

After university, Stephanie returned to Jamaica and became part of the family business. She became the managing director of the Bob Marley Foundation, Bob Marley Museum, Tuff Gong International, Tuff Gong Recordings, URGE,. and the Rita Marley Foundation. With this work Stephanie also fostered her father's legacy. Now living in Nassau in the Bahamas, Stephanie is directing the construction of the first Marley Resort and Spa. Although more attuned to the business end of things, Stephanie promoted concerts through Tuff Gong Productions and she stages the annual Reggae All-Star Concert in Nassau. In addition, Stephanie has four children, all boys.

The rest of the Marley children were fathered by Bob, but in relationships outside his marriage. Each child had a different mother; however, since Bob's death, Rita has become the mother figure to most of Bob's offspring. Bob had extramarital affairs with seven women who produced children. Some of his relationships were highly publicized, such as the "Beauty and the Beast" union with Cindy Breakspeare. Other child-producing encounters were fleeting and poorly documented, such as those with Evette Morris (Crichton) and Janet Hunt (Dunn). The children that were produced by these unions have been equally responsible for fostering their father's legacy and many of them have made their own deep impact on the music world.

ROHAN

Bob met Janet Hunt (or possibly Dunn) in the early 1970s. Janet was a dancer in a club and caught Bob's eye. Little was documented about their encounter; however, Janet gave birth to Bob's son Rohan as a result. Rohan Anthony Marley was born in May 1972, and his mother turned the boy over to Bob and Rita to raise when he was four. From this time,

Rohan officially became a Marley. He went to the same school as Ziggy and Stephen. Unlike his brothers, however, Rohan was more into sports than music. The Marley family had trouble keeping track of this active youth and he was sent to live with Bob's mother in Miami.

Cedella adopted Rohan and he flourished under her care. He graduated from Miami Palmetto Senior High School in 1991 and he enrolled at the University of Miami where he played linebacker for the Hurricanes football team. Rohan then had a short stint with the Ottowa Rough Riders professional football team in the Canadian Football League. After his time playing football, Rohan decided to settle down and refocus his energy.

More recently, Rohan married Lauryn Hill and began working in the Marley family businesses. For his part, Rohan preserves Bob's memory through his work with the Tuff Gong Clothing Company. Rohan styles clothes that are meant to have universal appeal, just like his father's music. In addition to his work with the clothing line, Rohan spends time with his own group of Bob's grandchildren. He has four children with Lauryn, sons Zion David, Joshua, and John, and a daughter named Selah Louise.

ROBERT (ROBBIE)

Bob's next child was born of his affair with a woman named Pat Williams. Williams was a woman from Trench Town and little is known of her. In fact, there are conflicting reports on her first name: some say Pat, some say Lucille. However, the story of her short time together with Bob was documented in his song "Midnight Ravers." The reports of the evening and the song itself described the scene. Bob had apparently been standing naked in the moonlit night at the house at 56 Hope Road. He was approached by Williams at that time and she seduced him. The next day, Bob woke up and wrote the lyrics to "Midnight Ravers" on a Kingston phone book. Robert Nesta Marley II, known as Robbie, was the product of this rendezvous.

Robbie, like many of the other children produced by Bob's affairs, came under the care of Rita. With Rita's and the Marley family's support, Robbie attended the University College of the West Indies, where he studied computer graphics. Since then, Robbie has been involved in several activities. He runs a clothing store in Miami, Florida, called Vintage Marley. He took up motorcycle riding and has subsequently become an accomplished stunt rider. This led him to a bit role in the 2003 movie, *2 Fast 2 Furious*. Additionally, he has a motorcycle riding club called the Miami Warriors. The Marley family tree continues to grow with Robbie's four children: Kaya, Ekitai, and twins Regal and Robert.

KAREN

Bob's tryst with a woman named Janet Bowen led to another Marley family child. Again, details on Janet are sketchy, but she is referred to as "Janet in England" in several sources. Janet gave birth to a daughter named Karen in 1973. Janet and Karen both remain shrouded in mystery, as neither has sought out the spotlight. Janet lived in Jamaica with her great-grandmother in Harbor View, St. Andrews. This is where she grew up and went to school. Her involvement with the Marley family has been slight. She was a reportedly a regular visitor to the Marley home in Kingston, but Karen did not fall in with the other children. When Bob's health failed, he asked Rita to look after Karen and she sent Karen to school with Stephanie. Because Karen has pursued a life outside the glare and scrutiny of the public eye, little else is known about her present life.

JULIAN

Lucy Pounder was a resident of Barbados and, while little is known of her time with Bob, it did produce Julian Marley on June 4, 1975. Julian was born and raised in London, but often spent time with Rita and the other Marley children in Jamaica and Miami. Following in this musical family's footsteps, Julian studied bass, drums, and keyboard from an early age. He also became an accomplished songwriter as a youth. His first single, at age five, was a version of his father's song "Slave Driver," recorded at the Marley family's Tuff Gong Studios in Kingston. This was just the first step in a busy and fruitful career.

In the 1990s, Julian asserted his musical strength at full potential. He formed his own band, called the Uprising band, and released the 1996 album *Lion in the Morning*. Julian was credited with writing or co-writing all of the songs on the album, which received critical acclaim. In his father's mold, Julian toured in support of the release and played internationally as a soloist backed by the Uprising band and as a member of Ghetto Youths International. As a member of Ghetto Youths, he interacted with his brothers Stephen and Damian and learned a great deal. With Damian, Julian opened for Ziggy Marley and the Melody Makers on the 1995 tour and was a featured artist on the 1999 Lollapalooza Festival Tour (which was quite a coup as this was a rock-oriented tour).

The new millennium found Julian ready for the next challenge. Julian worked with his Marley brothers to produce the platinum-selling *Chant Down Babylon* album, which paired modern artists with Bob from beyond

the grave. He was also a part of the "Master Blaster" Stevie Wonder tribute song with his brothers Stephen, Damian, and Ky-Mani. Julian's more
recent project was the 2003 album *Time and Place*. The sound of the album
was a mixture of roots reggae and light jazz. According to Julian himself,
the album was another step in his songwriting progression begun with
Lion in the Morning. With the conscious and politically charged lyrics of
his father and brothers ringing in his ears, Julian forwarded his Rastafarian and often militant messages. Also in keeping with the Marley family
mold, the songs on this release are a varied blend of reggae, funk, hip-hop,
and rhythm and blues.

The *Time and Place* album was produced by Julian, Stephen, and Damian. Ziggy and Rohan both appeared on the album, supplying percussion lines. Bob's old Wailers band compatriot, Bunny Wailer, also supplied
some percussion material. The Uprising band also appeared on the album.
In the wake of the release, Julian toured to support the album and the
Uprising band backed him up. Julian is outstanding among the Marley
children for his personality, presence, and musical talent. He applies his
energy tirelessly to the furthering of his father's musical legacy.

KY-MANI

Ky-Mani Marley was a product of the affair that Bob had with Anita
Belnavis. Belnavis was a well-known Caribbean table tennis champion.
Ky-Mani means "adventurous traveler" and so far that is exactly what he
has been. Belnavis's life went largely undocumented, but much is known
about her famous son. Ky-Mani Marley was born in Falmouth, Jamaica,
where he lived until age nine. At that time he moved to the inner city
of Miami, where he spent time engaged in sports. As a youth, he began
studying music, taking piano and guitar lessons, and he played trumpet in
his high school band. Although he studied music, his first love was sports
and he played high school football and soccer.

Growing up, Ky-Mani spent summers with his father, Rita, and the
other Marley children. In fact, in 1992, Ky-Mani moved to Jamaica to
be closer to the Marley family. His first excursion into music came while
he was still in Miami. He began rapping and DJ-ing and actually recorded
a single called "Unnecessary Badness." On his move back to Jamaica,
Ky-Mani dedicated himself to music. He worked with Stephen, Julian,
and Damian to produce his own musical product.

Early in his musical growth, Ky-Mani released several singles on the
Shang Records imprint. He did a version of "Judge Not" with dancehall
queen Patra, which was followed by the song "Dear Dad." This second

single was an open letter to his fallen father. Sentimental and thought provoking, "Dear Dad" was an early testament to Ky-Mani's songwriting ability. Picking up momentum, Ky-Mani teamed up with a third of the American band the Fugees when he worked with Praswell on a cover of the Eddy Grant hit "Electric Avenue." Major international exposure came when Ky-Mani performed at the Midem (short for *Marché international de l'édition musicale*), the world's largest music industry trade fair. His Midem performance was aired live by the Caribbean News Agency and Ky-Mani was instantly exposed to audience members in 36 countries.

Ky-Mani's international television appearance created unprecedented interest in the young singer. A label bidding war ensued, and Ky-Mani signed with Gee Street/V2 Records. For Gee Street, he teamed with P.M. Dawn on the single "Gotta Be Movin On Up," which only increased Ky-Mani's already rising stock. He further increased the interest in his music with the release of his 1999 solo debut album, *Ky-Mani Marley: Like Father Like Son*. This was followed the next year with *The Journey*, which illustrated beautifully Ky-Mani's versatile style. Moving between Spanish guitar, rock steady, and lovers rock, the songs on the album are as eclectic as Ky-Mani's taste.

The next album released by Ky-Mani was *Many More Roads* in 2001 Here the talented singer/songwriter presented material dipped in the roots reggae, dancehall, and rhythm and blues styles. Throughout this album, Ky-Mani delivered a message of consciousness and stayed true to his Rastafarian faith.

More recent projects found Ky-Mani trying his hand in show business. He played the lead role in the hit underground Jamaican movie *Shottas*, in which he worked opposite Wyclef Jean (of Fugees fame) and dancehall mainstay Spragga Benz. He also starred in the movie *One Love*, a romantic comedy that paired him with Cherine Anderson. In 2004, Ky-Mani landed another movie role, playing John the Baptist in the Frank E. Flowers movie *Haven*. Here the young Rasta played alongside Bill Paxton and Orlando Bloom. Ky-Mani remains enthusiastic about his role in maintaining Bob's musical fame. He has already done much to preserve the family name and further work is anticipated.

DAMIAN

Cindy Breakspeare was the woman most often associated with Bob apart from Rita. Breakspeare was from a white, upper-class background and was working in Kingston in the mid-1970s when she met Bob. As a teenager, she worked at the Kingston Sheraton and met Bob as they were both tenants in Blackwell's house at 56 Hope Road. At first, Bob and Breakspeare did not interact much. It was rumored that Bob made many attempts at gaining Breakspeare's affection, but she rebuked him. Bob's song "Waiting in Vain" was said to be about these rejected advances. However, as Bob's success increased, Cindy gradually warmed to his attention.

Breakspeare's rise to fame paralleled Bob's. A classic beauty, through the mid-1970s Breakspeare went from Miss Jamaican Bikini to Miss Universe Bikini to Miss World. She was also accused of being a home wrecker due to her association with Bob. However, history is clear that Bob pursued Breakspeare and early on she did not know that he was married. The period during which the two spent the most time was Bob's self-imposed exile from Jamaica after the assassination attempt.

Bob's interest in Breakspeare was somewhat contradictory to the philosophy of the rest of his life. Breakspeare was all things representing Babylon, in that she came from a wealthy white family and she surrounded herself with issues of vanity. As such, she was more concerned with winning beauty contests, such as Miss Jamaica Body Beautiful and Miss Universe Bikini, than with the plight of the black Jamaican underclass. However, Bob was not attracted to her only physically, but also because of her honesty. Because of this, Bob lavished attention on her that he did not on lavish any other woman. He bought her a house in the Cherry Gardens section of Kingston and gave her money to start her own business. Unlike his relationship with anyone other than Rita, when Bob and Breakspeare's sexual relationship ended they remained friends for the rest of Bob's life.

Breakespeare went on to marry jazz guitarist and pilot Rupert Bent. They live in the Stony Hill area of Jamaica and she remains busy. In addition to a singing career, through which she met her current husband, she maintains the Ital craft shop that Bob gave her the capital to start. Additionally, Cindy is the mother of Bob's son Damian "Junior Gong" Marley. Damian was born in 1978 in Jamaica and has carved out quite a niche in the Jamaican music industry. The Junior Gong is the youngest Marley child by any mother.

Like his brothers and sisters, Damian got an early start in music. He began performing at age 13 when he formed the Shepherds band. The group had local success and even performed at Reggae Bash in 1992 and at the 1992 installment of Reggae Sunsplash. Damian often performed around his older brothers and sisters as he frequently served as the opening act for Melody Makers concerts. By 1994, Damian was already working to establish a solo reputation. In 1996, he released his solo debut album,

Mr. Marley. Although it was a solo album, Damian's brother Stephen appeared on several songs and served as the producer. The release came out as an offering from the Ghetto Youths International label.

In 2001, Damian came into his own with his second solo record, *Half-way Tree.* The album earned the young singer a Grammy Award for the Best Reggae Album of the Year and saw Damian flexing his now powerful songwriting muscles. The biggest difficulty with the release was that it was largely ignored by the record-buying public. That all changed when Damian released *Welcome to Jamrock* in 2005. This release was afforded significant pre-release buzz and was immediately popular when it hit the streets. The title track came out in remixes and alternate versions right away, and the album made it into the Top 10. The album mixed hard-hitting lyrics about the realities of life with eclectic music that blended reggae, hip-hop, rhythm and blues, and dancehall.

Again it was a solo release, but Damian credited Stephen as the co-producer of the album. The production style is reminiscent of roots reggae stalwarts Sly and Robbie. The album was again released on the family's Tuff Gong/Ghetto Youths International label and revealed another of the Marley children coming into their own. In the light of his father's legacy, Damian's latest release mixed songs of protest with songs of love and again forwarded Bob's music and message.

Damian's most popular (and as yet most commercially viable) material echoed the sentiments of his father at his most militant. "Welcome to Jamrock" was a fiery and outraged description of the underprivileged held in bondage by the political system in Jamaica. This has not escaped the youngest Marley's attention. Damian has worked long and hard to make his music resonate on the streets and he has achieved that goal with his most recent offerings.

MAKEDA JAHNESTA

The last of the recognized Marley children was born in 1981. Makeda Jahnesta Marley was the product of an encounter between the reggae superstar and a woman named Yvette Crichton. Nothing was documented about this union beyond the notable product. The first name of the youngest of Bob's children was taken from the Bible and was also the Ethiopian name for the Queen of Sheba. Her middle name combines the Rastafarian word for God and her father's middle name. Makeda does not seem to have made a life in the limelight and little is known about her other than the fact that by 1992 she became an official beneficiary of the Marley estate and from that time forward was a regular at Rita's house.

RECENT DEVELOPMENTS

A particularly strange twist in Bob's life after death was announced in late 2006. Rita has planned a new Bob Marley biopic that will cover his life prior to his becoming famous. Oscar Award–nominated director Rachid Bauchareb (*Dust of Life*) has been tapped as the director. However, the biggest point of contention has been Rita's choice of Jamie Foxx to play the young Bob. While Foxx received critical acclaim for his portrayal of Ray Charles, it is unlikely that he can carry off a 16-year-old Marley. Due to this dubious choice, the film is already being heavily criticized and has only just gone into pre-production in early 2007.

And still the legend lives on. Beyond his fame, his legacy, his children, and his music, Bob's name itself continues to be praised and celebrated. The memory of the man continues to draw interest around the world. In fact, each year there are international concerts commemorating his birthday. Contrary to conventional wisdom (that eventually Bob will be forgotten), the concerts grow large and swell with more and more attendees annually.

One particularly interesting example was the celebration of Bob's 60th birthday in 2005. The official, and largest, celebration took place in Addis Ababa, Ethiopia, and was accompanied by a three-day conference about all things associated with Bob. Luminaries who were active in the conference included American actor Danny Glover, members of the Ethiopian government, Madame Winnie Mandela, Cedella Marley, Maya Angelou, India Irie, Ziggy Marley, and Angelique Kidjo. Performers who graced the stage during the celebration included Baaba Maal, Youssou N'Dour, Angelique Kidjo, Tagass King, and Rita and Ziggy Marley. The event centered on the conference in Ethiopia, but there were simultaneous celebrations around the world. The Bob Marley Foundation promoted 60th birthday events in the United States, Italy, Sweden, Germany, and South Africa.

The 2007 Bob Marley 62nd birthday celebration was another major event. For this, Stephen, Julian, Damian, and Ky-Mani staged a concert on February 10 called "Smile Jamaica." The concert was staged at the Marley ancestral home in Nine Mile, St. Ann Parish, Jamaica. The Marley sons took the concert's name from a like performance that their father gave in 1976. At that original concert, Bob was spreading the message of peace and now his sons have taken up that mission. The concert was purposely set to coincide with Bob Marley week, when the largest number of tourists visit Jamaica. With this, the joy and the message of Bob's life and music continue. His legacy is in the capable hands of his children and he is not forgotten. Robert Nesta Marley's music lives on in a variety of forms from Nine Mile to Kingston, from Miami to New York, from Jamaica to the rest of the world.

SELECTED DISCOGRAPHY

The Best of the Wailers 1970/Kong/Beverley's/BLP 001
> Soul Shakedown Party, Stop That Train, Caution, Soul Captives, Go Tell It on the Mountain, Can't You See, Soon Come, Cheer Up, Back Out, Do It Twice

Catch a Fire 1972 (April)/Marley and Blackwell/Island/ILPS 9241
> Concrete Jungle, Slave Driver, 400 Years, Stop That Train, Baby We've Got a Date, Stir It Up, Kinky Reggae, No More Trouble, Midnight Ravers

Burnin' 1973 (November)/Wailers and Blackwell/Island/ILPS 9256
> Get Up, Stand Up, Hallelujah Time, I Shot the Sheriff, Burnin' and Lootin', Put It On, Small Axe, Pass It On, Duppy Conqueror, One Foundation, Rasta Man Chant

African Herbsman 1973/Perry/Trojan/TRLS 62
> Lively Up Yourself, Small Axe, Duppy Conqueror, Trench Town Rock, African Herbsman, Keep On Moving, Fussing and Fighting, Stand Alone, All in One, Don't Rock My Boat, Put It On, Sun Is Shining, Kaya, Riding High, Brain Washing, 400 Years

Natty Dread 1974 (October)/Blackwell and the Wailers/Island/ILPS 9281
> Lively Up Yourself, No Woman, No Cry, Them Belly Full (But We Hungry), Rebel Music (Three O'Clock Road Block), So Jah Seh, Natty Dread, Bend Down Low, Talkin' Blues, Revolution

Live! Bob Marley and the Wailers 1975 (May)/Steve Smith and Blackwell/Island/ ILPS 9376
> Trench Town Rock, Burnin' and Lootin', Them Belly Full (But We Hungry), Lively Up Yourself, No Woman, No Cry, I Shot the Sheriff, Get Up, Stand Up

Rastaman Vibration 1976 (April)/Marley and the Wailers/ ILPS 9383
   Positive Vibration, Roots, Rock, Reggae, Johnny Was, Cry to Me, Want More, Crazy Baldhead, Who the Cap Fit, Night Shift, War, Rat Race
Exodus 1977 (May)/Marley and the Wailers/Island/ILPS 9498
   Natural Mystic, So Much Things to Say, Guiltiness, The Heathen, Exodus, Jamming, Waiting in Vain, Turn Your Lights Down Low, Three Little Birds, One Love/People Get Ready
Kaya 1978 (March)/Marley and the Wailers/Island/ILPS 9517
   Easy Skankin', Kaya, Is This Love, Sun Is Shining, Satisfy My Soul, She's Gone, Misty Morning, Crisis, Running Away, Time Will Tell
Babylon by Bus 1978 (December)/Marley and the Wailers/Island/ISLD 1298
   Positive Vibration, Punky Reggae Party, Exodus, Stir It Up, Rat Race, Concrete Jungle, Kinky Reggae, Lively Up Yourself, Rebel Music, War/No More Trouble, Is This Love, The Heathen, Jamming
Survival 1979 (October)/Marley, Wailers, and Alex Sadkin/ Island/ILPS 9542
   So Much Trouble in the World, Zimbabwe, Top Rankin', Babylon System, Survival, Africa Unite, One Drop, Ride Natty Ride, Ambush in the Night, Wake Up and Live
Uprising 1980 (June)/Marley and the Wailers/Island/ILPS 9596
   Coming in from the Cold, Real Situation, Bad Card, We and Dem, Work, Zion Train, Pimper's Paradise, Could You Be Loved, Forever Loving Jah, Redemption Song
Chances Are 1981/Sims, Nash, Perkins/Cotillion/SD 5228
   Reggae on Broadway, Gonna Get You, Chances Are, Soul Rebel, Dance Do the Reggae, Mellow Mood, Stay with Me, (I'm) Hurting Inside
Confrontation 1983/Blackwell and the Wailers/Island/7 90085–1
   Chant Down Babylon, Buffalo Soldier, Jump Nyabinghi, Mix Up, Mix Up, Give Thanks and Praises, Blackman Redemption, Trench Town, Stiff Necked Fools, I Know, Rastaman Live Up
Legend: The Best of Bob Marley 1984/Island/7 90169–1
   Is This Love, No Woman, No Cry, Could You Be Loved, Three Little Birds, Buffalo Soldier, Get Up, Stand Up, Stir It Up, One Love/People Get Ready, I Shot the Sheriff, Waiting in Vain, Redemption Song, Satisfy My Soul, Exodus, Jamming
Bob Marley and the Wailers: Rebel Music 1986/various producers/Island/ ILPS 9843
   Rebel Music, So Much Trouble in the World, Them Belly Full (But We Hungry), Rat Race, War, Roots, Slave Driver, Ride Natty Ride, Crazy Baldhead, Get Up, Stand Up
Bob Marley and the Wailers: The Birth of a Legend 1990/various producers/Epic/ ZGK 46769

Simmer Down, It Hurts to Be Alone, Lonesome Feelings, Love and Affection, I'm Still Waiting, One Love, I Am Going Home, Wings of a Dove, Let Him Go, Who Feels It Knows It, Maga Dog, I Made a Mistake, Lonesome Track, Nobody Knows, The Ten Commandments of Love, Donna, Do You Remember, Dancing Shoes, I Don't Need Your Love, Do You Feel the Same Way

Talkin' Blues 1991/Island-Tuff Gong/422–848 243

Talkin' Blues, Burnin' and Lootin', Kinky Reggae, Get Up, Stand Up, Slave Driver, Walk the Proud Land, Lively Up Yourself, You Can't Blame the Youth, Stop That Train, Rastaman Chant, Am-A-Do (previously unreleased)

Bob Marley: Songs of Freedom 1992/various producers/Island-Tuff Gong/TGCBX1

CD 1: Judge Not, One Cup of Coffee, Simmer Down, I'm Still Waiting, One Love, Put It On, Bus Dem Shut, Mellow Mood, Bend Down Low, Hypocrites, Stir It Up, Nice Time, Thank You Lord, Hammer, Caution, Back Out, Soul Shakedown Party, Do It Twice, Soul Rebel, Sun Is Shining, Don't Rock My Boat, Small Axe, Duppy Conqueror, Mr. Brown

CD 2: Screwface, Lick Samba, Trench Town Rock, Craven Choke Puppy, Guava Jelly, Acoustic Medley, I'm Hurting Inside, High Tide or Low Tide, Slave Driver, No More Trouble, Concrete Jungle, Get Up, Stand Up, Rastaman Chant, Burnin' and Lootin', Iron, Lion, Zion, Lively Up Yourself, Natty Dread, I Shot the Sheriff

CD 3: No Woman, No Cry, Who the Cap Fit, Jah Live, Crazy Baldhead, War, Johnny Was, Rat Race, Jammin', Waiting in Vain, Exodus, Natural Mystic, Three Little Birds, Running Away, Keep On Moving, Easy Skankin', Is This Love, Smile Jamaica, Time Will Tell

CD 4: Africa Unite, One Drop, Zimbabwe, So Much Trouble, Ride Natty Ride, Babylon System, Coming in from the Cold, Real Situation, Bad Card, Could You Be Loved, Forever Loving Jah, Rastaman Live Up, Give Thanks and Praise, One Love, Why Should I, Redemption Song

Bob Marley: I Shot the Sheriff 1993/live performance/On Stage CD/12037

(Recorded at the Quiet Knight Club, Chicago, June 10, 1975)

Trench Town Rock, Rebel Music, Natty Dread, Midnight Ravers, Slave Driver, Concrete Jungle, Talkin' Blues, I Shot the Sheriff

Bob Marley Interviews: So Much Things to Say 1995/RAS/various producers/RAS 3171

Natural Mystic, Trench Town Rock, Redemption Song, Babylon System, Time Will Tell, Natural Mystic, Revolution, Survival, One Drop, Roots, Rock, Reggae, Guava Jelly, Rat Race

Bob Marley and Friends: Roots of a Legend 1997/various producers/Trojan/ CDTAL 901

CD 1: Shocks of Mighty, part 1, Shocks of Mighty, part 2, Don't Let the Sun Catch You Crying, Upsetting Station, Zig Zag, Run for Cover, Long Long

Winter, All in One, Copasetic, One in All, More Axe, Shocks 71, The Axe Man, Send Me That Love, Man to Man, Nicoteen, Don't Rock My Boat, I Like It Like This, Love Light Shining, I Gotta Keep On Moving, Moving (alternative version), Rainbow Country

CD 2: Dreamland, Dreamland (version), Dreamland (version 2), The Crimson Pirate, Arise Blackman, Rightful Ruler, The Return of Alcapone, Maga Dog, Skanky Dog, Boney Dog, Downpresser, Moon Dust, Rudies Medley, Rude Boy (version), Dun Valley, Brand New Second Hand, Brand New Second Hand (version), Romper Room, Them a Fi Get a Beaten, Get a Beaten, Selassie Serenade, Leave My Business

The Complete Bob Marley and the Wailers, 1967–1972, Part 1 1997/Sims/JAD/ JAD-CD-1002

CD 1: Rock to the Rock, Rocking Steady, How Many Times, Touch Me, Mellow Mood, There She Goes, Soul Rebel, Put It On, Chances Are, Love, Bend Down Low, The World Is Changing, Nice Time, Treat You Right, What Goes Around Comes Around, What Goes Around Comes Around (version)

CD 2: Don't Rock My Boat, The Lord Will Make a Way, Chances Are, Selassie Is the Chapel, Tread Oh, Feel Alright, Rhythm, Rocking Steady, Adam and Eve, Wisdom, This Train, Thank You Lord, Give Me a Ticket, Trouble on the Road Again, Black Progress, Black Progress (version), Tread Oh (version)

CD 3: Sugar Sugar, Stop the Train, Cheer Up, Soon Come, Soul Captives, Go Tell It on the Mountain, Can't You See, Give Me a Ticket, Hold on to This Feeling, Mr. Chatterbox, Soul Shakedown (version), Soon Come (version), Mr. Chatterbox (version), Hold on to This Feeling (version)

The Complete Bob Marley and the Wailers, 1967–1972, Part II 1997/Sims/JAD/ JAD-CD-1004

CD 1: Try Me, It's Alright, No Sympathy, My Cup, Soul Almighty, Rebel's Hop, Corner Stone, 400 Years, No Water, Reaction. Dub tracks: My Sympathy, Soul Rebel (version), Try Me (version), It's Alright (version), No Sympathy (version), My Cup (version), Soul Almighty (version), Rebel's Hop (version), Corner Stone (version), No Water (version), No Water (version), Reaction (version), Rebel (version)

CD 2: Keep On Moving, Put It On, Fussing and Fighting, Memphis, Riding High, Kaya, African Herbsman, Stand Alone. Dub tracks: Brain Washing (version), Keep On Moving (version), Don't Rock My Boat (version), Fussing and Fighting (version), Put It On (version), Duppy (version), Memphis (version), Riding High (version), Kaya (version), African Herbsman (version), Stand Alone (version), Dun Is Shining (version), Brain Washing (version 2)

CD 3: Kaya, Love Light, Second Hand, Jah Is Mighty, Run for Cover, Man to Man, Downpresser, Don't Rock My Boat, More Axe, Long Long Winter, All in One, Turn Me Loose. Dub tracks: Kaya (version), Battle Axe (version), Long Long Winter (version), Second Hand (version); Downpresser (version), Shocks of Mighty (version), Axe Man (version), Nicoteen (version)

The Complete Bob Marley and the Wailers: 1967 to 1972, part III 1999/Sims/JAD/ JAD-CD-1005

CD 1: All in One (medley of Bend Down Low/One Love/Simmer Down/ Love and Affection), All in One (part 2: medley of Love and Affection/ Put It On), Keep On Skankin', Dreamland, Love Light, Brand New Second Hand (false start), Brand New Second Hand, Shocks of Mighty, Keep On Moving (also known as I'm Gonna Keep On Moving), Keep On Moving (extended version), Keep On Moving (extended version 2), Concrete Jungle, Screwface, Satisfy My Soul, Send Me That Love, Comma Comma, Jungle Dub (dub version of Concrete Jungle), Dracula (dub version of Mr. Brown), Love Light (dub version), Dreamland (dub version), Face Man (dub version of Screwface), Satisfy My Soul (dub version)

CD 2: Screwface, Redder Than Red, Lively Up Yourself, Trouble Dub, Dub Feeling, Satisfy My Soul, Kingston 12, Pour Down the Sunshine, Gonna Get You, Cry to Me, Reggae on Broadway, I'm Hurting Inside, Oh Lord, Got to Get There, Dance Do the Reggae, Stay with Me, Guava Jelly, Guava (dub version of Guava Jelly), Red (dub version of Redder Than Red), Live (dub version of Lively Up Yourself), Samba (dub version of Lick Samba), Screwface (dub version), Grooving Kingston (dub version of Trench Town Rock), Choke (dub version of Craven Chock Puppy), Satisfy My Soul (dub version)

Bob Marley and The Wailers: The Complete Soul Rebels and the Upsetter Record Shop 1999/Lee Perry/Culture Press/CP 017

CD 1: Soul Rebels, Soul Rebels (version), No Water, No Water (version), Rebel Hop, Rebel Hop (version), No Sympathy, No Sympathy (version), It's Alright, It's Alright (version), Reaction, Reaction (version), Corner Stone, Corner Stone (version), 400 Years, 400 Years (version), Make Up, Make Up (version), Try Me, Try Me (version), Soul Almighty, Soul Almighty (version)

CD 2: Concrete Jungle, Concrete Jungle (version), Screwface, Screwface (version), Love Life, Love Life (version), Satisfy My Soul, Satisfy My Soul (version), Rainbow Country, Rainbow Country (version), Long Long Winter, Long Long Winter (version), Put It On, Put It On (version), Don't Rock My Boat, Don't Rock My Boat (version), Keep On Movin', Keep On Movin' (version)

Bob Marley and the Wailers: Climb the Ladder 2000/Dodd/Heartbeat/11661–7751–2

Dancing Shoes, Put It On, Lonesome Track, Climb the Ladder, Love Won't Be Mine This Way, Dreamland, Lemon Tree, Nobody Knows, Wings of a

Dove, Sinner Man, Ten Commandments of Love, Sunday Morning, I Made a Mistake, I Don't Need Your Love, Donna, The Jerk, Just in Time

Bob Marley and the Wailers: Catch a Fire (Deluxe Edition) 2001/Marley and Blackwell/UMe/314548635–2

CD 1: Concrete Jungle, Stir It Up, High Tide or Low Tide, Stop That Train, 400 Years, Baby, We've Got a Date, Midnight Ravers, All Day, All Night, Slave Driver, Kinky Reggae, No More Trouble

CD 2: Concrete Jungle, Slave Driver, 400 Years, Stop That Train, Baby, We've Got a Date, Stir It Up, Kinky Reggae, No More Trouble, Midnight Ravers

Bob Marley and the Wailers: Exodus (Deluxe Edition) 2001/Marley and Blackwell/UMe /314586408–2

CD 1: Natural Mystic, So Much Things to Say, Guiltiness, The Heathen, Exodus, Jamming, Waiting in Vain, Turn Your Lights Down Low, Three Little Birds, One Love/People Get Ready

Additional tracks: Roots, Waiting in Vain (alternate version), Jamming (long version), Jamming (version), Exodus (version)

CD 2: The Heathen, Crazy Baldhead/Running Away, War/No More Trouble, Jamming, Exodus, Punky Reggae Party, Punky Reggae Party (version), Keep On Moving, Keep On Moving (version), Exodus

Bob Marley and the Wailers: Rastaman Vibration (Deluxe Edition) 2002/Marley and Blackwell/UMe /440063446–2

CD 1: Positive Vibration, Roots, Rock, Reggae, Johnny Was, Cry to Me, Want More, Crazy Baldhead, Who the Cap Fit, Night Shift, War, Rat Race

Additional tracks: Jah Live, Concrete Jungle, Roots, Rock, Reggae (version), Roots, Rock Dub, Want More, Crazy Baldhead (version), Johnny Was

CD 2: Introduction, Trench Town Rock, Burnin' and Lootin', Them Belly Full (But We Hungry), Rebel Music, I Shot the Sheriff, Want More, No Woman, No Cry, Lively Up Yourself, Roots, Rock, Reggae, Rat Race, Smile Jamaica Sessions (late 1976), Smile Jamaica (part one), Smile Jamaica (part two)

Bob Marley and the Wailers: Live at the Roxy 2003/Suha Gur/UMe /B0000516–02

Introduction, Trench Town Rock, Burnin' and Lootin', Them Belly Full (But We Hungry), Rebel Music, Want More, No Woman, No Cry, Lively Up Yourself, Roots, Rock, Reggae, Rat Race

Encore: Positive Vibration, Get Up, Stand Up/No More Trouble/War

Bob Marley and the Wailers: Burnin' (Deluxe Edition) 2004/Marley and Blackwell/UMe /B0003359–02

CD 1: Get Up, Stand Up, Hallelujah Time, I Shot the Sheriff, Burnin' and Lootin', Put It On, Small Axe, Pass It On, Duppy Conqueror, One Foundation, Rasta Man Chant

Bonus tracks: Reincarnated Souls, No Sympathy, The Oppressed Song, Get Up, Stand Up (unreleased alternate take), Get Up Stand Up (unreleased single version)

CD 2: Duppy Conqueror, Slave Driver, Burnin' and Lootin', Can't Blame the Youth, Stop That Train, Midnight Ravers, No More Trouble, Kinky Reggae, Get Up, Stand Up, Stir It Up, Put It On, Lively Up Yourself

Africa Unite: The Singles Collection 2005/Marley and Blackwell/Island/ B0005723–02

Soul Rebels, Lively Up Yourself, Trench Town Rock, Concrete Jungle, I Shot the Sheriff, Get Up, Stand Up, No Woman, No Cry, Roots, Rock, Reggae, Exodus, Waiting in Vain, Jammin', Is This Love, Sun Is Shining, Could You Be Loved, Three Little Birds, Buffalo Soldier, One Love/People Get Ready, Africa Unite, Slogans, Stand Up/Jamrock

Bob Marley and the Wailers: Gold 2005/Marley and Blackwell/Island/B0004008–02

CD 1: Stir It Up, Slave Driver, Concrete Jungle, Get Up, Stand Up, I Shot the Sheriff, Burin' and Lootin', Lively Up Yourself, Rebel Music, Trench Town Rock, No Woman, No Cry, Jah Live, Positive Vibration, Roots, Rock Reggae, Crazy Baldhead, Natural Mystic, Exodus, Jammin'

CD 2: One Love/People Get Ready, Waiting In Vain, Punky Reggae Party, Is This Love, Sun Is Shining, Satisfy My Soul, Kinky Reggae, Medley: War/No More Trouble, So Much Trouble in the World, Africa Unite, One Drop, Could You Be Loved, Coming in from the Cold, Redemption Song, Buffalo Soldier, Rastaman Live Up, Iron, Lion, Zion

One Love at Studio One: 1964–1966 2006/Marley/Heartbeat/CBHBEA319

CD 1: This Train, Simmer Down, I Am Going Home, Do You Remember, Mr. Talkative, Habits, Amen, Go Jimmy Go, Teenager in Love, I Need You, It Hurts to Be Alone, True Confessions, Lonesome Feelings, There She Goes, Diamond Baby, Playboy, Where's the Girl for Me, Hooligan Ska, One Love, Love and Affections, Tell The Lord

CD 2: And I Love Her, Rude Boy, I'm Still Waiting, Ska Jerk, Somewhere to Lay My Head, Wages of Love (rehearsal), Wages of Love, I'm Gonna Put It On, Cry to Me, Jailhouse, Sinner Man, He Who Feels It Knows It, Let Him Go, When the Well Runs Dry, Can't You See, What Am I Supposed to Do, Rolling Stone, Bend Down Low, Freedom Time, Rocking Steady

Bob Marley: The Anthology 2006/various/Golden Lane Records/1580

CD 1: Natural Mystic, Rainbow Country, I Know A Place, Concrete Jungle, Trench Town Rock, Sun Is Shining, Keep On Skanking, Satisfy My Soul, Keep On Moving, Long Long Winter, Don't Rock My Boat, Dr. Brown, My Cup, Love Light Shining, Who Colt the Game

CD 2: Lively Up Yourself, Small Axe, More Axe, Duppy Conqueror, Kaya, Kaya (version), Turn Me Loose, Soul Rebel, Run for Cover, Picture on the

Wall, African Herbsman, Man to Man, Jah is Mighty, Stand Alone, Send Me That Love

The Very Best of Bob Marley 2006/various/Mastersong/B000FFJ7EU

CD 1: African Herbsman, Lively Up Yourself, Fussing and Fighting, Soul Rebel, Soul Shakedown, 400 Years, Sun Is Shining, Natural Mystic, Soul Almighty, Kaya, Reaction, No Sympathy, Mellow Mood, Trench Town Rock, Cheer Up, Small Axe, Rebel's Hop, Caution, Rainbow Country, Can't You See

CD 2: All in One, There She Goes, My Cup, It's Alright, Treat You Right, Mr. Brown, Brain Washing, Stand Alone, Corner Stone, Duppy Conqueror, Chances Are, Put It On/Don't Rock My Boat, You Can't Do That to Me, Hammer, No Water

Bob Marley Forever 2006/various/Madacy Records/B000JMK68U

CD 1: Rebel's Hop, Soul Almighty, Trench Town Rock, African Herbsman, Stand Alone, Mr. Brown, Brain Washing, 400 Years, All in One, Caution, Soon Come, Go Tell It on the Mountain

CD 2: Kaya, Soul Rebel, It's Alright, My Cup, Mellow Mood, Touch Me, No Water, Soul Captives, Don't Rock My Boat, Try Me, Rainbow Country, Fussin' and Fightin'

CD 3: How Many Times, Memphis, Riding High, Corner Stone, Hammer, You Can't Do That to Me, Chances Are, Stop the Train, Duppy Conqueror, Lively Up Yourself, Sun Is Shining, Do It Twice

Bob Marley and the Wailers: Trilogy 2006/various/Music Brokers Arg/B000F2BNYK

CD 1: There She Goes, Can't You See, Cheer Up, Back Out, Satisfy My Soul, Redder Than Red, Mellow Mood, Soul Shakedown Party, Mr. Brown, Soul Captives, Go Tell It on the Mountain, Soon Come, Do It Twice, Stop the Train, Mr. Chatterbox, Power and More Power, Touch Me, Treat You Right

CD 2: Try Me, It's Alright, No Sympathy, My Cup, Soul Almighty, 400 Years, No Water, Reaction, Keep On Moving, Don't Rock My Boat, Put It On, Riding High, Riding High, Kaya, Sun Is Shining, Concrete Jungle, Screw Face, Love Life

CD 3: Lively Up Yourself, Rainbow Country, Natural Mystic, Small Axe, Fussin' and Fightin', Corner Stone, Chances Are, Caution, Hammer, Rebels Hop, All in One (medley), Soul Rebel, Trench Town Rock, You Can't Do That to Me, How Many Times, Brain Washing, Duppy Conqueror, Rasta (instrumental), I Shot the Sheriff (instrumental), Try Me (instrumental)

Bob Marley: 400 Years 2006/various/Dbk Works/B000EUMK8Q

Soul Shakedown Party, Lively Up Yourself, Trench Town Rock, Stand Alone, Fussin' and Fightin', Memphis, Brain Washing, Duppy Conqueror, Riding High, Reaction, Soul Almighty, Sun Is Shining, Small Axe, All in One (medley), 400 Years, Mr. Brown

Bob Marley: Reggae Master 2006/various/Immergent/B000I0N6PE
    Lively Up Yourself, Trench Town Rock, African Herbsman, Kaya, Stand
    Alone, Soul Rebel, 400 Years, It's Alright, No Sympathy, Rebel's Hop, Cor-
    ner Stone
Bob Marley: No Sympathy 2006/various/Dbk Works/B000EUMK86
    Kaya, Rainbow, Soul Rebel, African Herbsman, Try Me, It's Alright, There
    She Goes, You Can't Do That To Me, Touch Me, Hammer, My Cup, Chances
    Are, Treat You Right, No Water, Corner Stone
Bob Marley: Stop That Train 2006/various/Dbk Works/B000CC4VZ6
    Natural Mystic, Keep On Moving, Soul Captives, How Many Times, Stop
    That Train, Go Tell It on the Mountain, Caution, Back Out, Mellow Mood,
    Rebel's Hop, Do It Twice, Put It On, Don't Rock My Boat, Cheer Up, Soon
    Come, Can't You See
Bob Marley: Soul Shakedown Party 2006/various/Ground Floor/B000FBG0JO
    CD 1: Soul Shakedown Party, Small Axe, Back Out, Do It Twice, Trench
    Town Rock, Natural Mystic, 400 Years, Mr. Brown, Soul Rebel, Rainbow
    Country, Kaya, Keep On Moving, Don't Rock My Boat, Put It On, There
    She Goes, Mellow Mood, Chances Are, Hammer, You Can't Do That to Me
    CD 2: African Herbsman, Stand Alone, Sun Is Shining, Brain Washing,
    Lively Up Yourself, Go Tell It on the Mountain, Duppy Conqueror, Fussin'
    and Fightin', Riding High, Try Me, No Sympathy, My Cup, Corner Stone,
    No Water, Reaction, Cheer Up, Soon Come, Rebel's Hop, Put It On, Soul
    Captives
Bob Marley: Keep On Skanking 2006/various/Atom/B000EHTO3I
    Satisfy My Soul, Don't Rock My Boat, Kaya, 400 Years, Duppy Conqueror,
    Jah Is Mighty, Keep On Moving, Screw Face, This Train, Soul Rebel, All In
    One, Go Tell It on the Mountain, African Herbsman, Hey, Happy People,
    Picture on the Wall, Corner Stone, Soul Shakedown Party, Trench Town
    Rock, Thank You Lord, Lively Up Yourself, Small Axe, Concrete Jungle, Put
    It On, Keep On Skanking, My Cup, Rainbow Country, Dracula, Long Long
    Winter, Mr. Brown, Natural Mystic, I Like It Like This, Stop That Train,
    Wisdom, Nicoteen, Man to Man, Sun Is Shining
Bob Marley and the Wailers: Definitive Gold 2006/various/Déjà vu Italy/
    B000IMV3ZQ
    Trench Town Rock, Soul Rebel, Kaya, Go Tell It on the Mountain, Try Me,
    It's Alright, No Sympathy, No Water, Rainbow Country, There She Goes,
    Mellow Mood, Treat You Right, Chances Are, Hammer, Touch Me, Caution,
    Soul Captives, Can't You See, Reaction, 400 Years, Natural Mystic, Lively
    Up Yourself, Soul Shakedown Party, Soon Come, Cheer Up, Back Out, Do
    It Twice, Keep On Moving, Don't Rock My Boat, Put It On, Fussin' and
    Fightin', Duppy Conqueror, Small Axe, Riding High, African Herbsman,

Stand Alone, Sun Is Shining, Mr. Brown, Stir It Up, Stop That Train, Keep On Skanking, Brain Washing, Corner Stone, All in One, Man to Man, Wisdom, Mr. Chatterbox, One in All, Dreamland, Run for Cover, I Like It Like This, Turn Me Loose, Brand New Second Hand, This Train, There She Goes, How Many Times, Treat You Right, Love Light Shining, Rebel's Hop, Satisfy My Soul, Picture on the Wall, Shocks of Mighty, Shocks of Mighty (part 2), My Cup, Adam and Eve, Downpressor, Long Long Winter, Thank You Lord, Tell Me, Soul Almighty, Send Me That Love, Make Up, Concrete Jungle, Screw Face, Love Life, Nice Time, Power and More Power, Redder Than Red, Hypocrites, All in One/One Love, Sun Is Shining Dub, No Sympathy Dub, Kaya Dub, Concrete Jungle Dub, Soul Rebels Dub, No Water Dub, 400 Years Dub, Don't Rock My Boat Dub, Corner Stone Dub, Soul Almighty Dub, Rebel's Hop Dub, It's Alright Dub, Keep On Movin' Dub, Rainbow Country Dub, Satisfy My Soul Dub, Fussin' and Fightin' Dub, African Herbsman Dub, Duppy Conqueror Dub, Dracula/Mr. Brown Dub

BIBLIOGRAPHY

BOOKS AND ARTICLES

Balford, Henry. "Marley's Legacy Lives On, But…" *Jamaica Observer*, February 26, 2004, n.p.

Barrett, Leonard. *The Rastafarians: The Dreadlocks of Jamaica*. Boston, MA: Beacon Press, 1988.

Barrow, Steve, and Peter Dalton. *Reggae: The Rough Guide*. New York: Penguin Books, 1997.

Bennett, Scotty. *Bob Marley*. New York: Virgin Publishing, 1997.

Booker, Cedella, and Anthony Winker. *Bob Marley: An Intimate Portrait by His Mother*. New York: Viking, 1996.

Boot, Adrian, and Vivian Goldman. *Bob Marley—Soul Rebel—Natural Mystic*. London: Eel Pie Publisher, 1981.

Boot, Adrian, and Michael Thomas. *Jamaica: Babylon on a Thin Wire*. London: Thomas and Hudson, 1976.

Bordowitz, Hank, ed., *Every Little Thing Gonna Be Alright: The Bob Marley Reader*. Cambridge, MA: Da Capo Press, 2004.

Bradley, Lloyd. "Uprising." *Mojo*, March 2005, 69–81.

Bramwell, Osula. "'Redemption Song': Protest Reggae and Jamaica." PhD diss., University of Waterloo, Canada, 1984.

Burnett, Michael. *Jamaican Music*. London: Oxford University Press, 1982.

Campbell, Horace. *Rasta and Resistance: From Marcus Garvey to Walter Rodney*. Trenton, NJ: Africa World Press, 1987.

Campbell, Howard. "Jamming with Jimmy Norman." *Jamaica Observer*, November 22, 2002.

Campbell, Howard. "Reggae Icon Remembered." *Jamaica Gleaner,* February 7, 2005.

———. "The Wailers Band: Still Rockin' in the Nineties." *Reggae Report* 14, no. 4 (April 1996): 24–25.

Cassidy, Frederic Gomes, and R. B. Le Page. *Dictionary of Jamaican English.* 2nd ed. Mona, Jamaica: University of the West Indies Press, 2003.

Chevannes, Barry. *Rastafari: Roots and Ideology.* New York: Syracuse University Press, 1994.

Cooke, Mel. "Marley Museum Now Official Heritage Site." *Jamaica Gleaner,* February 7, 2005.

Cooper, Carolyn. "Chanting Down Babylon: Bob Marley's Song as Literary Text." *Jamaica Journal* 19, no. 4 (November 1986): 2–8.

Dalrymple, Henderson. *Bob Marley: Music, Myth, and the Rastas.* Sudbury, UK: Carib-Arawak, 1976.

Davis, Stephen. *Bob Marley.* New York: Doubleday, 1985.

———. *Bob Marley.* Reprint, Rochester, VT: Schenkman Books, 1990.

———. *Bob Marley: Conquering Lion of Reggae.* London: Plexus, 1994.

Davis, Stephen, and Peter Simon. *Reggae Bloodlines: In Search of the Music and Culture of Jamaica.* New York: Da Capo Press, 1992.

———. *Reggae International.* New York: Alfred A. Knopf, 1983.

Dawes, Kwame. *Bob Marley: Lyrical Genius.* London, UK: Sanctuary Publishing Limited, 2002.

Dolan, Sean. *Bob Marley.* Philadelphia: Chelsea House Publishers, 1996.

Farley, Christopher, *Before The Legend: The Rise of Bob Marley.* New York: HarperCollins, 2006.

———. "How Marley Caught Fire: Repackaging the Reggae King as a Rock Star Helped Sell His Music to the World." *Wall Street Journal,* April 27, 2006.

Fricke, David. "Blackwell Remembers." *Rolling Stone,* no. 969, March 10, 2005, 78.

Furgusson, I. "'So Much Things to Say': The Journey of Bob Marley." *Village Voice* 27 (May 18, 1982): 39–43.

Gilmore, Mikal. "The Life and Times of Bob Marley: How He Changed the World." *Rolling Stone,* no. 969, March 10, 2005, 68–78.

Goldman, Vivian. *The Book of Exodus: The Making and Meaning of Bob Marley's Album of the Century.* New York: Three Rivers Press, 2006.

Gray, Obika. *Radicalism and Social Change in Jamaica, 1960–1972.* Knoxville: University of Tennessee Press, 1991.

Hausman, Gerald. ed. *The Kebra Nagast: The Lost Bible of Rastafarian Wisdom and Faith from Ethiopia and Jamaica.* New York: St. Martin's Press, 1997.

Henke, James. *Marley Legend: An Illustrated Life of Bob Marley.* San Francisco: Chronicle Books, 2006.

Howard, Dennis. "Professor Rex Nettleford on the Creative Power of Bob Marley." *Reggae Report* 14, no. 4 (April 1996): 20–21.

Jaffe, Lee. *One Love: Life with Bob Marley and the Wailers*. New York: W. W. Norton, 2003.

Jensen, Richard J. "Bob Marley's 'Redemption Song': The Rhetoric of Reggae and Rastafari." *Journal of Popular Culture* 29, no. 3 (Winter 1995): 17–20.

Lacey, Terry. *Violence and Politics in Jamaica, 1960–1970*. Manchester, UK: Manchester University Press, 1977.

Lee, Peter. "Glory to Jah: Remembering Bob Marley." *Guitar Player* 25, no. 5 (May 1991): 82–87.

Lipsitz, George. *Dangerous Crossroads*. New York: Verso, 1994.

Manuel, Peter. *Caribbean Currents: Caribbean Music from Rumba to Reggae*. Philadelphia: Temple University Press, 1995.

Marley, Bob. "A Conversation with Bob Marley." Interviewer's name unknown. Reprinted as "Bob Marley's 1979 Interview." *The Beat* 18, no. 3 (1999): 40–43.

Marley, Cedella, and Gerald Hausman, eds. *60 Visions: A Book of Prophesy by Bob Marley*. Miami, FL: Tuff Gong Books, 2004.

May, Chris. *Bob Marley*. London: Hamish Publishers, 1985.

McCann, Ian. *Bob Marley in His Own Words*. New York: Omnibus Press, 1993.

———. *The Complete Guide to the Music of Bob Marley*. New York: Omnibus Press, 1994.

McKenzie, Clyde. "Bob Marley: For the People." *Reggae Report* 14, no. 4 (April 1996): 13.

Moskowitz, David. *Caribbean Popular Music: An Encyclopedia of Reggae, Mento, Ska, Rock Steady, and Dancehall*. Westport, CT: Greenwood, 2005.

———. *The Words and Music of Bob Marley*. Westport, CT: Praeger, 2007.

Mulvaney, Rebekah M., and Carlos Nelson. *Rastafari and Reggae: A Dictionary and Source Book*. Westport, CT: Greenwood, 1990.

Murrell, Nathanial, ed. *Chant Down Babylon: The Rastafari Reader*. Philadelphia: Temple University Press, 1998.

National Library of Jamaica. *Marley Bibliography*. Kingston, Jamaica: National Library of Jamaica, 1985.

Nettleford, Rex. *Caribbean Cultural Identity: An Essay in Cultural Dynamics*. Kingston, Jamaica: William Collins and Sangster, 1970.

———. *Mirror Mirror: Identity, Race, and Protest in Jamaica*. Kingston, Jamaica: William Collins and Sangster, 1970.

Patterson, Orlando. *Children of Sisyphus*. London: Longman, 1964.

Perone, James. *The Key of Life: The Words and Music of Stevie Wonder*. Westport, CT: Praeger, 2006.

Potash, Chris. *Reggae, Rasta, Revolution: Jamaican Music from Ska to Dub*. New York: Schirmer Books, 1997.

Rockwell, John. "Marley, Wailers Dig Into Reggae Roots." *New York Times*, June 20, 1975, A, 25.

Rodney, Walter. *The Groundings with My Brothers*. London: Bogle-L'Ouverture, 1969.

Rosen, Craig. "Marley's 'Legend' Lives on in 1984 Island Set," *Billboard* 108, no. 47 (November 23, 1996): 13–18.

Sheridan, Maureen. *The Story behind Every Bob Marley Song: 1962–1981*. New York: Thunder's Mouth Press, 1999.

Sinclair, Tom. "The Legend of Bob Marley." *Entertainment Weekly*, no. 806, February 11, 2005, 6–10.

Smith, M. G. *Culture, Race, and Class in the Commonwealth Caribbean*. Mona, Jamaica: University of the West Indies Press, 1984.

Stephens, Roger. "Bob Marley: Rasta Warrior." In *The Rastafari Reader: Chant Down Babylon*, edited by Nathaniel Murrell, William Spencer, and Adrian McFarlane. Philadelphia: Temple University Press, 1998.

Talamon, Bruce W. *Bob Marley: Spirit Dancer*. New York: W. W. Norton, 1994.

Taylor, Don. *Marley and Me: The Real Bob Marley Story*. New York: Barricade Books , 1995.

———. *So Much Things To Say: My Life as Bob Marley's Manager*. New York: Blake Publishers, 1995.

Wagner, Charles R. "Jah as Genre: The Interface of Reggae and American Popular Music." PhD diss., Bowling Green University, 1993.

Warner, Keith Q. "Calypso, Reggae, and Rastafarianism: Authentic Caribbean Voices." *Popular Music and Society* 12, no. 1 (Spring 1988): 53–62.

White, Garth. *The Development of Jamaican Popular Music with Special Reference to the Music of Bob Marley*. Kingston, Jamaica: African-Caribbean Institute of Jamaica, 1982.

White, Timothy. *Catch a Fire: The Life of Bob Marley*. Rev. ed., New York: Henry Holt and Company, 1994.

Whitney, Malika, and Dermott Hussey. *Bob Marley: Reggae King of The World*. Kingston, Jamaica: Kingston Publishers, 1984.

Winders, J. A. "Reggae, Rastafarians, and Revolution: Rock Music in the Third World." *Journal of Popular Culture* 17, no. 1 (January 1983): 62.

WEB SITES

Each of these sites was consulted in the authoring of the encyclopedia. Reference dates are inconsequential, as each site was visited repeatedly over the period of January 2004 to January 2005. All URLs have been verified and only "official" artist and label Web sites were consulted.

Artists Only Records. *Reggae Artists.* http://www.artistsonly.com/reggae.htm.

BBC Music. http://www.bbc.co.uk/cgi-perl/music/muze/index.

Black Music Collectors. http://www.black-music-collectors.com/labels/uscata logue.htm.

Bob Marley Music, Inc. *Life of Bob Marley.* http://www.bobmarley.com/life/.

Clarke, Donald. *MusicWeb Encyclopaedia of Popular Music.* http://www.musicweb. uk.net/encyclopaedia/.

Crazy Baldhead. *Artist Index.* http://www.geocities.com/SunsetStrip/Disco/6032/ main.htm.

Davis, Stephen. *Bob Marley Biography.* http://www.grovemusic.com/date/articles/ music/2/230/23065.xml.

Gleaner Company Limited. *Jamaica Daily Gleaner.* http://www.jamaica-gleaner.com.

IReggae. http://www.ireggae.com/reggae1.htm.

JAD Records: Where the Legend Began. http://www.jadrecords.com/.

Jimmy Cliff Music. *Biography.* http://www.jimmycliffonline.com.

Lee "Scratch" Perry Music. http://www.upsetter.net/scratch/.

Peter Tosh Music. *The Man: His Story.* http://www.ptosh.com/story.html.

Reggae Movement. *Players, Singers, Spinners.* http://www.reggaemovement.com/ rm1/artists.htm.

Reggae Seen. http://www.reggaeseen.com/artists/.

Reggae Train. *Artists.* http://www.reggaetrain.com/site_artists.asp.

Roots Archive. http://www.roots-archives.com.

Taj Mahal Music. *Biography and Discography.* http://www.taj-mo-roots.com/ discography/bio.html.

Teacher and Mr. T. Reggae Vibes Productions. http://www.reggae-vibes.com.

Toots and the Maytals Music. *Extended Biography.* http://www.tootsandthemaytals. net/toots/tootsbiographylong.aspx.

Trojan Records. Main. http://www.trojanrecords.net.

Tuff Gong Studios. Jamaica: Studio, Manufacturing, Distribution, and Record Shop. http://www.tuffgong.com/.

Universal Music Group. *Artist Index: Bob Marley and the Wailers.* http://new.umusic. com/Artists.aspx?Index=1.

INDEX

(Song titles in quotes, album titles in italics)

"Terror," 9

"Them Belly Full," 26, 30, 35, 68

Third World Band, the, 38–39, 41, 54

Thompson, Dennis, 34

"Three Little Birds," 41–42, 91

"Time Will Tell," 48

Top Gear, 23

Top of the Pops, 43, 48

"Top Rankin'," 53

Tosh, Peter, 8, 10, 12, 15–16, 19–21, 23–27, 31, 34, 46, 55, 80, 82

Tower Theater, Philadelphia, 35

Treasure Isle studios, 9

"Trench Town," 6, 8, 10, 33, 95

Trinity, 46

Tull, Jethro, 20

"Turn Your Lights Down Low," 41–42

Twelve Tribes of Israel, 16, 34, 45–46, 61, 70, 74–75

"Two Sevens Clash," 40

Uniques, the, 12

Uprising, 55–57, 59–60, 64–65, 68

Upsetter Records, 18

Upsetters, 18

Wailer, Bunny. *See* Livingston, Neville

Wailing Wailers, 10–12

Wail'N Soul'M, 16–18

"Waiting in Vain," 41–42, 81, 99

"Wake Up and Live," 53–54

"Want More," 34–35

"War," 34–35, 39, 47, 49, 63, 68, 81, 95

"We and Dem," 59

"What's New Pussycat," 12

"Who the Cap Fit," 34

Williams, Patricia, 22

Wilmington, Delaware, 10, 14, 92

Winwood, Steve, 20, 40

Wonder, Stevie, 31, 55, 89, 92, 97

"Work," 59–60, 68

Wright, Betty, 58

Yesuhaq, Archbishop, 74

Zap Pow horns, 25, 39, 42

"Zimbabwe," 54, 62

Zimbabwe (Africa), 54, 57, 62–64, 68, 89

Zimbabwe African National Union (ZANU), 62

"Zion Train," 59, 68

Zurich, Switzerland, 64

About the Author

DAVID V. MOSKOWITZ is associate professor of musicology and graduate coordinator in music at the University of South Dakota. He is the author of the Greenwood reference book *Caribbean Popular Music: An Encyclopedia of Reggae, Mento, Ska, Rock Steady, and Dancehall* and *The Words and Music of Bob Marley*, which is part of The Praeger Singer-Songwriter Collection.